What Life Was Like®

DURING THE AGE OF REASON

France
AD 1660 – 1800

What Life Was Like

DURING THE AGE OF REASON

France
AD 1660 ~ 1800

BY THE EDITORS OF TIME-LIFE BOOKS, ALEXANDRIA, VIRGINIA

CONTENTS

During the Age
of Reason

PHILOSOPHERS AND KINGS

In 1784 when Immanuel Kant tried to sum up the era known as the Enlightenment, the great philosopher came up with a simple motto: "Dare to know! Have the courage to use your own reason!" The period in which Kant lived was, indeed, a time of reason—and of daring. All across Europe, and even in the distant American colonies, writers and scholars were challenging traditional certainties about the authority of kings, the structure of the universe, even the very existence of God. Unquestioning obedience to religious, political, and social authority began to be supplanted by the scrutiny of ideas under the penetrating light of reason.

New ways of thinking about the world led to efforts to transform it. Determined to create a freer and more humane society, reformers advocated religious tolerance; an end to torture, serfdom, and slavery; a freer economy; the expansion and modernization of education; the elimination of censorship; the extension of political representation; and the protection of individual rights. And over time the people in France responded: They rose up to threaten the rule, the extravagance—and the life—of their king.

The men who planted the seeds of these revolutionary ideas came from a variety of backgrounds and traditions. The leaders of the French Enlightenment included Montesquieu, a nobleman, magistrate, and wine grower; Voltaire, who emerged from the ranks of the wealthy bourgeoisie; and Jean-Jacques Rousseau, a watchmaker's son in exile from Geneva. Out-

| 1643 - 1715 | 1685 | 1687 | 1690 | 1715-1774 | 1740-1786 |

1643 - 1715 — Louis XIV, the Sun King, rules France

1685 — Revocation of the Edict of Nantes by Louis XIV leads to renewed persecution of French Protestants

1687 — Isaac Newton publishes *Principia Mathematica*

1690 — John Locke publishes *Essay Concerning Human Understanding*

1715-1774 — Reign of Louis XV of France

1740-1786 — The philosopher king Frederick the Great rules Prussia

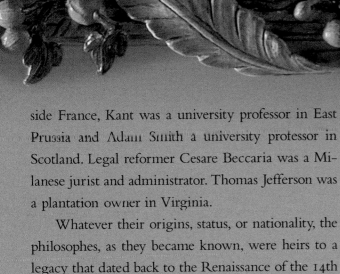

side France, Kant was a university professor in East Prussia and Adam Smith a university professor in Scotland. Legal reformer Cesare Beccaria was a Milanese jurist and administrator. Thomas Jefferson was a plantation owner in Virginia.

Whatever their origins, status, or nationality, the philosophes, as they became known, were heirs to a legacy that dated back to the Renaissance of the 14th and 15th centuries. During that great era of European rebirth and renewal, scholars had become reacquainted with the classical civilizations of Greece and Rome. Drawing from the ancient texts, they had developed a new humanist philosophy that broke with the medieval focus on God and centered all intellectual pursuit on the study of man.

Though faith still held sway in the 16th century, a time that spawned such Protestant reformers as Martin Luther and John Calvin, scholars undertook ever more precise observation of the world around them. In 1543 Polish astronomer Copernicus shocked the church with the heretical suggestion that the sun, not the earth, was the center of God's universe. The Italian scientist Galileo would expand the work of Copernicus, challenging the traditional principles of astronomy laid down by Ptolemy in Alexandria 1,500 years before and advancing the proposition that the book of nature was written in mathematical language.

Seventeenth-century thinkers built on these foundations. But they did so without relying on the ancient texts so revered by the Renaissance humanists or on the scriptures so important to the Protestant reformers. In England, Francis Bacon sought to purge intellectual inquiry of inherited notions and to increase knowledge of the natural world through ob-

1740-1748	1745-1764	1748	1751-1772	1756-1763	1759

War of the Austrian Succession

Montesquieu publishes *The Spirit of Laws*

Seven Years' War pits France and Austria against Prussia in Europe and France against England in North America

Madame de Pompadour exercises influence as mistress to Louis XV

Diderot publishes the *Encyclopédie*

Voltaire publishes *Candide*

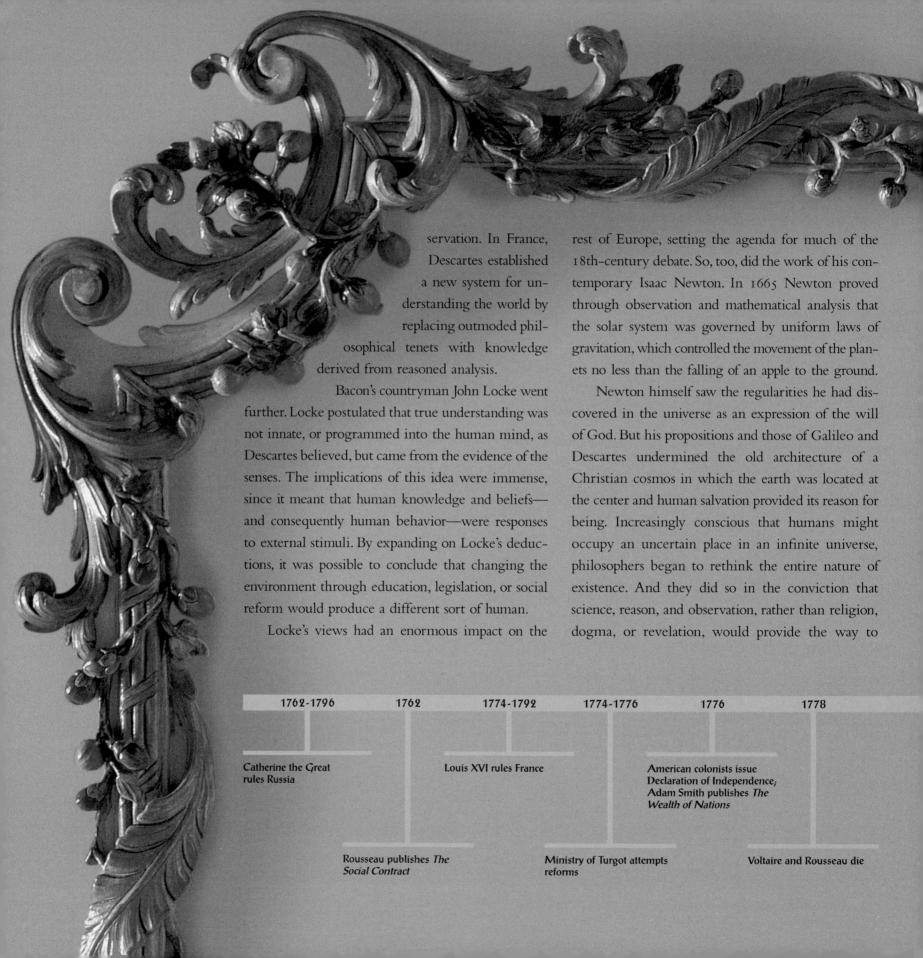

servation. In France, Descartes established a new system for understanding the world by replacing outmoded philosophical tenets with knowledge derived from reasoned analysis.

Bacon's countryman John Locke went further. Locke postulated that true understanding was not innate, or programmed into the human mind, as Descartes believed, but came from the evidence of the senses. The implications of this idea were immense, since it meant that human knowledge and beliefs—and consequently human behavior—were responses to external stimuli. By expanding on Locke's deductions, it was possible to conclude that changing the environment through education, legislation, or social reform would produce a different sort of human.

Locke's views had an enormous impact on the rest of Europe, setting the agenda for much of the 18th-century debate. So, too, did the work of his contemporary Isaac Newton. In 1665 Newton proved through observation and mathematical analysis that the solar system was governed by uniform laws of gravitation, which controlled the movement of the planets no less than the falling of an apple to the ground.

Newton himself saw the regularities he had discovered in the universe as an expression of the will of God. But his propositions and those of Galileo and Descartes undermined the old architecture of a Christian cosmos in which the earth was located at the center and human salvation provided its reason for being. Increasingly conscious that humans might occupy an uncertain place in an infinite universe, philosophers began to rethink the entire nature of existence. And they did so in the conviction that science, reason, and observation, rather than religion, dogma, or revelation, would provide the way to

1762-1796	1762	1774-1792	1774-1776	1776	1778

Catherine the Great rules Russia

Louis XVI rules France

American colonists issue Declaration of Independence; Adam Smith publishes *The Wealth of Nations*

Rousseau publishes *The Social Contract*

Ministry of Turgot attempts reforms

Voltaire and Rousseau die

useful truths, placing their emphasis on life on earth instead of life after death.

Newton would have been shocked by some of the conclusions the philosophes reached. Nevertheless, as science advanced in the period following his discoveries—the age now declared by the philosophes to be the century of enlightenment, the *siècle des lumières*—religion was compelled to retreat.

Nowhere was this spirit of enlightenment, this climate of daring, more evident than in France, the most powerful country in Europe in the 1700s. As we shall see in the chapters ahead, France was ruled by the kings of the House of Bourbon: Louis XIV, under whom absolute monarchy reached its height; Louis XV, whose rule spanned most of the century; and Louis XVI, whose claim to absolute rule ended in crisis.

In the final years of Louis XVI's reign, the pressure for change became irresistible as ministers seeking to save the monarchy from total collapse began a process of reform they proved powerless to control. Reform turned into revolution in 1789 as an assembly called by the monarch abruptly seized power in the name of the nation. The French Revolution began with a declaration of the rights of man and of citizens, largely inspired by the philosophes' program of reason, freedom, and equality. But as the revolution took a more radical turn, killing the king, launching the new republic into war with its neighbors, and escalating repression within its own borders, the siècle des lumières gave way to the Reign of Terror. Unable to secure itself, the republic that had replaced the absolute monarchy would itself be replaced by the imperial rule of Napoleon Bonaparte. The Age of Enlightenment was over; the Age of Revolution and War had begun.

1781	1787-1789	1789	1793	1793-1794	1799-1815

Immanuel Kant publishes
Critique of Pure Reason

French Revolution begins;
Declaration of the Rights of
Man and of the Citizen;
Lavoisier publishes *Elementary Treatise on Chemistry*

The Reign of Terror

French government
endeavors to save the
monarchy from bankruptcy

Execution of Louis XVI and
Marie-Antoinette

Napoleon Bonaparte
rules France

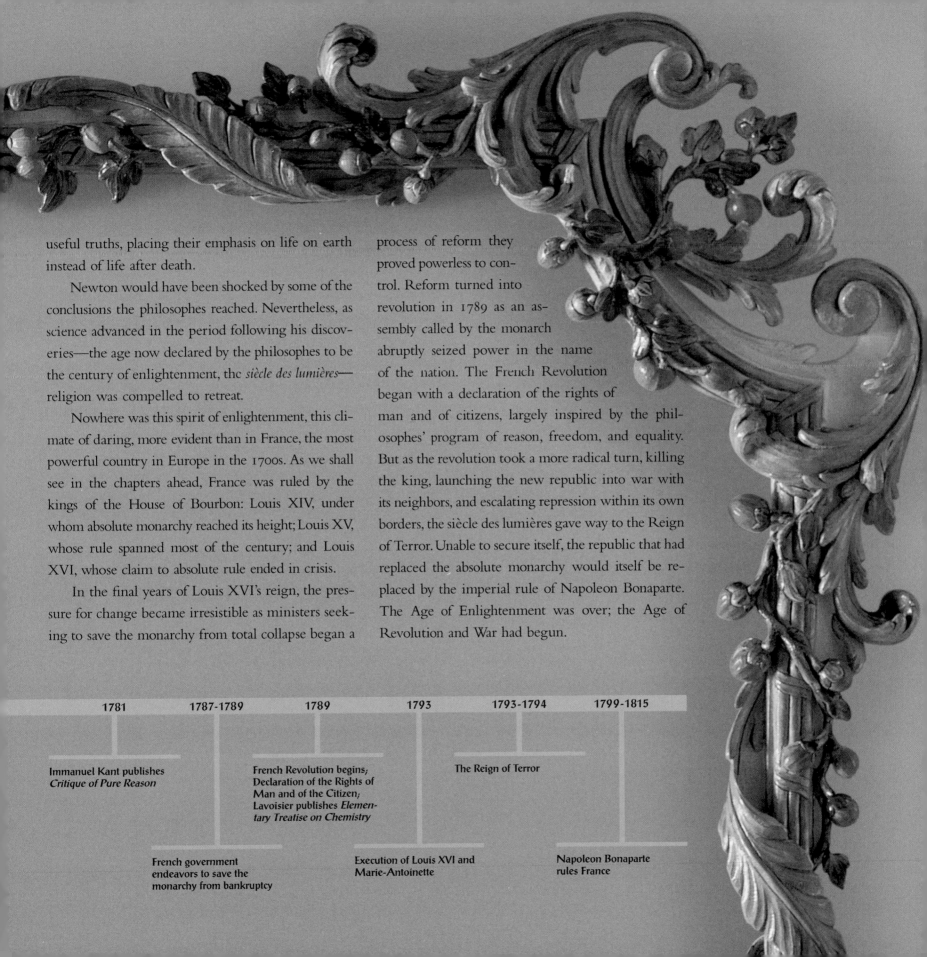

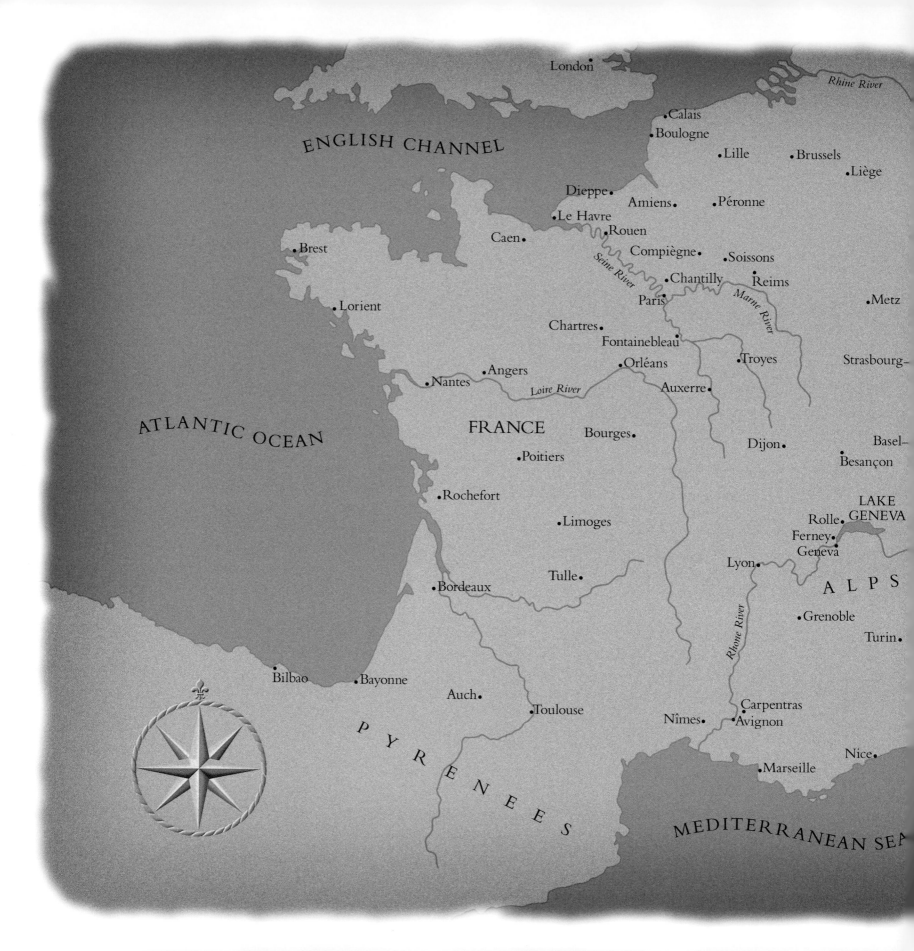

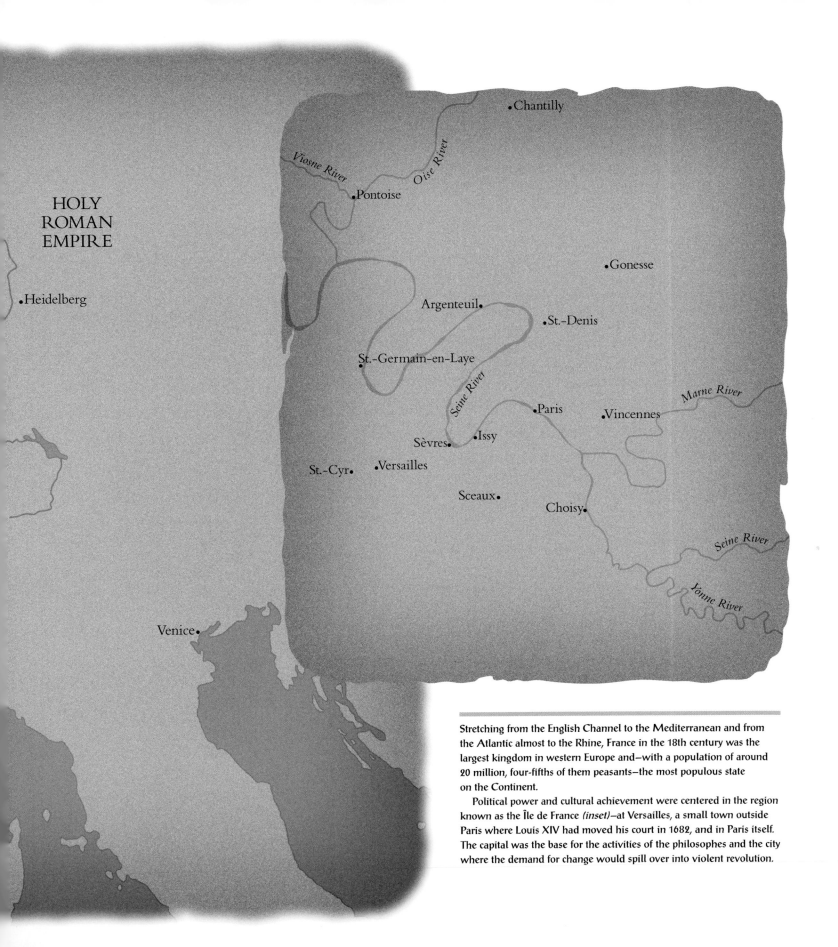

HOLY
ROMAN
EMPIRE

Heidelberg

Chantilly

Viosne River

Oise River

Pontoise

Gonesse

Argenteuil

St.-Denis

St.-Germain-en-Laye

Seine River

Marne River

Paris

Vincennes

Sèvres

Issy

St.-Cyr

Versailles

Sceaux

Choisy

Seine River

Venice

Yonne River

Stretching from the English Channel to the Mediterranean and from the Atlantic almost to the Rhine, France in the 18th century was the largest kingdom in western Europe and—with a population of around 20 million, four-fifths of them peasants—the most populous state on the Continent.

Political power and cultural achievement were centered in the region known as the Île de France *(inset)*—at Versailles, a small town outside Paris where Louis XIV had moved his court in 1682, and in Paris itself. The capital was the base for the activities of the philosophes and the city where the demand for change would spill over into violent revolution.

The Sun King

Over the course of his 72-year reign, Louis XIV attempted to establish an absolute monarchy in France. Named king in 1643 as a boy of four, Louis assumed full power in 1661. From then on, nothing in his kingdom was unworthy of his attention, no detail too small for him to consider. Until his death in 1715, he sought to exercise control of his realm in every aspect, from war to religion, from public works to fashion trends.

Louis moved his court to Versailles from Paris to escape the unruly city and to concentrate France's social and political hierarchy around him. Over a period of five decades and at enormous expense, architects, decorators, and landscape designers turned Versailles into one of the most exquisite seats of government ever constructed. There, while devoting himself to the task of governing, Louis also provided entertainment without equal and established France as the cultural center of Europe for the next century.

During his reign, Louis XIV did much to advance his nation. But the Enlightenment flourished, in part, because it represented an alternative to his despotism and profligacy. And though many decried his excesses, Voltaire noted later, "His name can never be pronounced without respect and without summoning the image of an eternally memorable age."

Likening himself to the center of the universe, Louis XIV used a sunburst *(left)* as his personal emblem throughout Versailles *(right),* the lavish palace complex he built on the site of his father's hunting lodge. A portrait by Hyacinthe Rigaud *(below)* painted in 1701 shows off the aging king's shapely legs; Louis studied ballet for some 20 years and was an accomplished court dancer.

A Ruler's Private Life

After the death of his father, Louis XIII, young Louis was left in the care of his mother, Anne, who acted as his regent. Though nominally king of France and, hence, semidivine, he was given over to servants to be raised. Their attitude toward their charge seems neglectful at best, and at one point in his childhood, he was allowed to wander alone and nearly drowned in a pond.

The young king fell in love several times before dutifully marrying Marie-Thérèse of Austria, daughter of the king of Spain, assuring peace between their countries for a time. The loveless marriage produced six children, only one of whom lived to adulthood. That child, Louis's eldest son, was known as the dauphin, or crown prince, and his grandson would become Louis's successor.

As he went about his daily life at Versailles, playing the lead role in a very public spectacle, the king still was able to steal away from his official duties for an hour or two each day to engage in extramarital rendezvous. Each of his paramours accepted the fact of his simultaneous involvement with other women, though not with pleasure. Louise de La Vallière, an officer's daughter who shared his love of riding, became his first official mistress. The marquise de Montespan, an intelligent and engaging woman, succeeded her. Both bore him many children, of whom he was very fond; he eventually made them legitimate.

His longest-lasting love was Madame de Maintenon, governess to marquise de Montespan's children; Louis secretly married Maintenon after the queen's death. Before that, though, when both mistresses, along with the queen, were ensconced in rooms conveniently near the king, Madame de Maintenon allegedly passed the marquise on the queen's staircase, quipping, "You are going down, Madame? I am going up."

An allegorical painting of Louis XIV and his family portrays him sitting cross-legged to the right of his mother (center). His brother and sister-in-law are seated at far left, his queen, Marie-Thérèse, is at his left hand. Louis's mistresses (above, top to bottom) included Madame de Maintenon; Louise de La Vallière; and the marquise de Montespan, mother of his favorite son.

The Glory of Versailles

"Every day is one long round of dances, ballets, comedies, music of all kinds, . . . promenades, hunts and other entertainments," wrote Jean-Baptiste Colbert about Versailles. Colbert, the king's finance minister, was not proclaiming its pleasures, but rather was protesting the huge expenditures for the palace and the lifestyle of its inhabitants, saying it detracted from the king's glory.

The monarch, a master of public relations, knew otherwise. Versailles, a glittering world with a palace large enough to house thousands and filled with glass, tapestries, marble, and lace beyond compare, would enhance both his and France's prestige in Europe. Soon, heads of state were traveling from all over to marvel at the most dazzling court in the most beautiful place on the Continent.

France's peasants shouldered the burden of paying for such splendor, and Louis destroyed his financial records to avoid a furor over his extravagance. But it was noted that the estate's 1,500 fountains used more water than the city of Paris and that upon command, gardeners would replace flower beds so that Louis would not see the same view twice.

"Love conquers all" is the theme of this medieval-style tournament pitting gentlemen against ladies. Versailles's fabulous days-long fetes amazed the rest of Europe.

Louis XIV dances the role of the sun god Apollo in a ballet. Fond of performing, he was instrumental in popularizing classical dance.

The king pursues his favorite pastime of hunting stag, wolf, and boar on the palace grounds.

Near the end of his life, the wheelchair-bound king and his entourage pause by the Apollo Fountain and the Grand Canal during his daily outing.

Patron of Arts and Sciences

Louis XIV's desire to shape public opinion extended beyond the world's perception of his new capital. He also sought to influence France's history, literature, art, and science. To accomplish this goal, he used a system of royal patronage to financially bind the era's cultural and intellectual figures to his court. Once an artist began receiving a state pension, for example, the king felt entitled to determine the style and subject matter of his work.

This system may also have encouraged and stimulated creative endeavors; Louis's reign coincided with one of the most magnificent periods in French cultural history. The seemingly bottomless well of funds available for the building of Versailles furnished endless employment for some of the greatest talents of the age: architect Louis Le Vau, artist Charles Le Brun, landscape designer André Le Nôtre, and sculptor François Girardon. Literary giants Molière and Racine provided plays, and Jean-Baptiste Lully produced French operas for the court's amusement.

Louis did not confine his patronage to Versailles. He had painters and historians escort him to battles, to record his actions for posterity. And he established, in Paris, a series of academies, among them dance, science, architecture, and music, to study and to disseminate information of all kinds and, not least, to add to the glory of the king.

A tapestry shows Louis XIV visiting the Gobelin factory, a government-run enterprise he set up to produce furnishings for his palaces.

Italian sculptor Giovanni Bernini's commission to create a bust of Louis XIV signaled a shift from Italy to France as Europe's cultural center.

Louis XIV's greatest minister, Jean-Baptiste Colbert, at left in this painting by Henri Testelin, presents members of the newly created Academy of Sciences to the king in 1667.

"L'État, C'Est Moi"

Throughout his reign, Louis XIV attempted to embody his most famous dictum, "L'état, c'est moi," or "The state, it is I." At the age of 22, he declared sovereignty was to be his alone; by the time he died, 54 years later, he had nearly achieved his goal.

The king, a Roman Catholic and self-styled Defender of the Faith, saw himself as God's representative on earth, and nonbelievers as both sinners and rebels. Determined to quash rebellion in all forms, Louis first tried to force French Protestants to convert, then brutally expelled many who refused, destroying between 600 and 700 Huguenot churches in the process.

As the so-called Powerful Ruler, Louis acted as his own principal minister, representing France at home and abroad. He served as head of state, first diplomat, and chief bureaucrat.

Louis, the "Victorious Warrior," inspired his men by accompanying them on campaigns. But his relentless warfare left the country broke. On his deathbed, looking back, he advised his great-grandson, the future Louis XV: "Try to remain at peace with your neighbors. I have loved war too much. Do not copy me in that, or in my overspending. Lighten your people's burden as soon as possible, and do what I have had the misfortune not to do myself."

A symbolic representation portrays Louis XIV as Defender of the Faith revoking the Edict of Nantes *(left),* a decree that had provided limited religious toleration of Protestantism.

A fanciful rendition of Louis on horseback being crowned by Fame *(right)* supports his image as the semidivine Victorious Warrior.

At a sumptuous reception in the Hall of Mirrors, the Persian ambassador presents himself to the Powerful Ruler as the soon-to-be Louis XV watches.

CHAPTER ONE

"After Us, the Deluge"

Dressed in his coronation robes, the boy king Louis XV strikes a regal pose in this state portrait of 1715. Although the five-year-old orphan was painfully shy and frail, he survived to rule France for nearly 60 years and, for a time at least, was given the sobriquet "Louis the Beloved."

In a gilded chamber within the great palace of Versailles, a little boy named Louis clenched his fists tightly, opened his mouth, and began to wail. Tears streamed out of the corners of his eyes, leaving silver trails on his cheeks.

The stricken five-year-old stared at the knot of grim-faced men who looked down upon him from the doorway. They were the mightiest grandees of France, royal dukes and princes of the blood, yet they saluted him with the deepest and most deferential of bows. Behind them he could see a mob of lesser courtiers jostling each other and craning their necks. At their head stood his great-uncle, the duc d'Orléans, waiting for the storm of sobs to subside. "Your Majesty," murmured the duke. "Please, Sire . . ."

The words triggered another tearful explosion. For, although little more than a toddler, Louis knew exactly what this new form of address portended: His ancient and ailing great-grandfather had finally, after months of suffering, slipped away. Now he, the Sun King's tiny, trembling namesake, found himself transformed into Louis XV of France.

Fate—in the shape of a measles epidemic and a physician whose remedies proved more lethal than the disease—had already deprived him of his mother, father, and older brother. By his second birthday, Louis was heir to the throne. His great-grandfather had kept a watchful eye on the little orphan's progress and, when death approached, given the boy his blessing. But the span of 72 years between them, and the manners of the time, made intimacy almost impossible. For warmth and affection little Louis depended on his governess, the duchesse de Ventadour. No one touched him as closely: He even called her Maman.

He was lucky to have her. When he fell ill with the same sickness that had killed his parents, Madame de Ventadour snatched Louis out of the grasp of the royal doctor with his ruthless regimens of bloodletting and purges; her doubts about these therapies almost certainly saved her charge's life. The maintenance of his health became a sacred trust. She supervised his exercise and diet, made sure his clothes were light or warm

During the eight years of Louis XV's minority, Philippe, duc d'Orléans, governed France as regent in league with a regency council, seen below at one of its sessions. In practice, however, council meetings were a mere formality and real power lay with the regent.

enough to suit the weather, and kept a close watch on every aspect of his routine.

In obedience to Louis XIV's last wishes, Madame de Ventadour also taught his heir how to comport himself as king. She armed him with three golden rules: He was to serve God, to behave with the majesty and decorum that befitted his exalted position, and to conceal his true emotions under a bland and regal mask. Little Louis proved an apt pupil.

Until the new monarch reached the age of wisdom, his great-uncle Philippe, the duc d'Orléans, would govern France as regent. But Louis was not exempt from all royal responsibilities. On September 12, 1715, just 11 days after the old king's death, he made his first ceremonial appearance before the peers of the realm, officially confirming the regent's powers and inaugurating the new reign.

The grave little boy did not put a foot wrong as he ascended the long staircase to his throne. Close behind him came the duc de La Trémoille, First Gentleman of the Bedchamber, holding the monarch's long train. Once seated, Louis addressed the gathering: "Gentlemen, I have come here to assure you of my affection for you. My Chancellor will tell you what I have decided."

For a full hour the five-year-old king sat still, managed not to fidget, and apparently listened as intently as any of the scarlet-robed dignitaries before him. Occasionally, suffering from the heat of the chamber and the weight of his own robes, he reached out for the handkerchief that Madame de Ventadour held ready, wiped his face, and passed it back again.

The regent, aware that he was molding the mind of a king, encouraged the child to attend the councils of state. Louis came to the meetings shyly clutching his pet cat, or as the ministers called it, his "colleague." He sat in silence, stroking the creature's silky coat as he watched his elders govern the realm in his name.

In his 13th year Louis was deemed mature enough to receive the crown. A grand coronation at Reims cathedral on October 25, 1722, was followed, four months later, by a solemn coming-of-age ceremony before the judges and lawyers of the Parlement of Paris, the most powerful of the royal courts of law. The regent retired. Officially his work was done. But behind the scenes Louis's ministers and councilors still ruled France, under the control of the king's 21-year-old cousin, the ambitious duc de Bourbon, universally known as Monsieur le Duc.

The adolescent Louis remained a closed book even to his nearest relatives. "Our King," remarked his great-aunt, the old duchesse d'Orléans, "is a very handsome and very pleasant young man, but he is too silent. When he doesn't know people intimately, one can get nothing out of him."

The king's innermost thoughts and feelings might stay secret, but nothing else about him did. Virtually every aspect of his daily life was a public spectacle, conducted under his courtiers' fascinated gaze. On some occasions even the contents of his chamber pot became a subject for public discussion. The whole court, for instance, worried when their young sovereign suffered an unpleasant bout of constipation. Everyone applauded when the royal physician announced that he had administered a laxative, which, he declared, had caused "a charming evacuation."

Every waking moment, from the king's morning ablutions to his bedtime prayers, was governed by an elaborate etiquette. For shy Louis this strict routine served as both a place of safety and a prison.

The first royal rite of the day was the king's *lever*. In this ceremony, Louis's chief valet opened His Majesty's bed curtains, His Majesty rose to greet the day, and the highest nobles of the realm—in strict order of rank—entered the State Bedchamber to greet His Majesty.

Since the State Bedchamber was as drafty as it was magnificent, the king never slept there. Instead he spent his nights in a more modest but more comfortable chamber. Sometimes he was up and about for hours, waking early and lighting the fire himself rather than rousing the servants to brave the cold on his behalf. "I would rather let the poor people sleep," he confessed to one astonished nobleman. "I keep them awake often enough."

Louis might sometimes behave unconventionally in the treatment of his servants, but he always followed palace protocol. So, at the appointed hour, he would proceed to his official bedchamber, dutifully lie down, and close the bed curtains around himself. The *lever,* the opening act in the drama of the king's day, could now begin.

At the officially designated moment of waking, the doors opened to admit the princes of the blood—direct descendants of earlier kings of France—and certain intimates of long standing. The moment when Louis's feet touched the floor signaled the arrival of the First Gentleman of the Bedchamber. The next rank of nobles had to wait until the king eased his arms into his dressing gown. Only when he sat down in an armchair to be groomed and powdered was the common herd of courtiers free to enter.

The king's meals—apart from informal suppers with a handful of his closest friends—were consumed in a virtual goldfish bowl. He breakfasted and lunched at a table set for one, with every mouthful monitored by dozens of pairs of eyes. When he prayed, his entourage followed him to the royal chapel, where a set of complex social rituals required at least as much attention as the Mass itself.

At night, the last act in the ritual drama of the royal day, the *coucher,* was played out when His Majesty retired—officially, though not always literally—for the night. As in the morning, access to the State Bedchamber was a heatedly sought-after privilege. Inside the room itself, lifelong enmities could be kindled between those who jockeyed for positions that would bring them closest to the person of the king. But only princes of the blood and the holders of a few exalted offices—the Grand Chamberlain, the First Gentleman of the Bedchamber, or the Grand Master of the Wardrobe—were deemed worthy to hand the monarch his nightclothes.

No prize was more avidly pursued than the right to hold the royal candlestick and light the king's way to bed. When everyone else was shooed out of the State Bedchamber, only the recipient of this honor—chosen nightly—was allowed to remain. A shrewd courtier could use this moment of unprecedented intimacy to make an impres-

Described by a visiting German as "one of the handsomest princes in Europe," Louis never lacked for mistresses. Yet he was devoted to his family and, continued the visitor, "his behavior and his feelings are those of a virtuous man." Although Louis enjoyed socializing, he shunned the hedonistic lifestyle led by many nobles.

Queen Marie Leszczyńska, shown here in a 1748 portrait, dutifully bore the king 10 children. But she was seven years older than Louis and too plain and pious to continue to attract his attention and affection. The queen spent most of her time sewing, praying, and sponsoring charitable works.

sion, stand out from the crowd, and ingratiate himself with his royal master. It was an assignment coveted by any ambitious nobleman, for the king granted favors only to people he knew.

Once the candle was snuffed out and its delighted carrier dismissed, Louis would leave the chilly State Bedchamber for more comfortable quarters—a suite of 50 rooms and seven bathrooms, known as the Petits Appartements, open only to a handful of envied guests. Yet not even this palace-within-the-palace could satisfy Louis's craving for privacy. In the course of his reign he would transform the entire north wing of Versailles into a warren of secret passages, hidden staircases, secluded courtyards, and tiny but luxuriously appointed rooms available for reflection, rest, and discreet encounters.

But despite his best efforts, Louis had no escape from prying eyes. As the boy king ripened into a handsome youth, his courtiers developed a keen, not to say obsessive, interest in his sexual development. When Louis was just 14 his chief minister, Monsieur le Duc, and the duke's mistress, the marquise de Prie, tried to steer him toward various attractive young ladies. But Louis stayed resolutely immune to their temptations. Undeterred, the marquise made it her business to find the young king a bride. This concern for his happiness hid an ulterior motive: If Louis died without an heir, the crown passed to her paramour's archrival, the duc d'Orléans, son of the now-deceased regent. Madame de Prie was impatient for Louis to marry and beget as many sons as necessary to keep the Orléans branch of the royal family from taking over the throne.

The marquise soon found the ideal candidate: Princess Marie Leszczyńska, the 21-year-old daughter of the dethroned king Stanislaw of Poland. The young lady's father might have fallen victim to the turbulent politics of central Europe, but her blood remained a suitably royal shade of blue. Although Europe boasted other theoretically eligible princesses, each one had certain disadvantages. One was Protestant; another from a noble house too friendly with France's Austrian rivals; a third disqualified because of a supposed tendency by her mother to give birth to hares.

Marie Leszczyńska might not shine for her intelligence or her looks—indeed, in comparison to the bright and beautiful creatures who adorned Versailles she seemed dull and downright dowdy—but she had many virtues. She was kind, mild mannered,

A ROOM FOR THE AGES

At the very heart of the palace of Versailles, the Hall of Mirrors has been called one of the greatest architectural achievements in the world. Designed during the reign of Louis XIV, it consists of three distinct areas: the Salon de la Guerre (Salon of War) at one end of the hall, the Salon de la Paix (Salon of Peace) at the other end, and the 250-foot marble arcade that links them.

Adorning the hall's 40-foot-tall vaulted ceiling are a series of paintings depicting coronations, treaties, and various military victories—"an unbroken chain of marvelous deeds," according to the dramatist Racine, the king's official historian. Down one side of the hall, 17 large arched windows overlook the palace's magnificent gardens and fountains, a view beautifully reflected in the matching Venetian mirrors that line the opposite interior wall.

During the daytime, the Hall of Mirrors—the

Galerie des Glaces—was abuzz with activity. Sedan chairs bearing ministers traversed the hall, conveying individuals to various destinations within the palace. Officials on court business bustled to and fro along the arcade. The king's official bedchamber was located just behind the wall of mirrors, and he would have entered the hall every day. There, he might receive ambassadors from England, Spain, or Sweden, as well as envoys from such distant lands as Turkey, Persia, and Siam.

But at night, after the sun had set outside the 17 west-looking windows, the Hall of Mirrors attained its full glory as a venue for royal wedding feasts, state banquets, or costume balls. In crystal chandeliers suspended from the ceiling and free-standing candelabra held aloft by statues of straining attendants, thousands of candles illuminated the hall, their light reflected in the mirrors to wondrous effect and producing a setting fit for the kings and queens of France.

31

dutiful, and pious. And, in Madame de Prie's eyes, the princess possessed an even greater asset: her potential gratitude. For the daughter of a deposed and impoverished monarch, a match with the glorious Louis XV would seem an impossible dream. If this dream came true, she would forever remain indebted to the lady who had made her queen of France.

Louis, encouraged by Monsieur le Duc and the marquise, agreed to the match. This led to some diplomatic unpleasantness, since the king was, at the time, formally engaged to a seven-year-old Spanish princess. While Louis, at 15, had reached an age deemed suitable for marriage, the little *infanta* obviously had not. But even a king's health could be fragile; there was no time to waste.

behind the gilded doors. Would the king, until now famously immune to feminine charms, succeed in performing his marital obligations? The next morning Louis emerged with a glint in his eye. He seemed to have discovered a new interest in life. Monsieur le Duc and the marquise de Prie breathed a sigh of relief.

As a means of prolonging the dynasty, the marriage was clearly a success. In the space of little more than a decade Marie bore two sons—the desired heir and a spare—as well as eight daughters. But it soon became evident that once outside the bedroom Louis and Marie had little in common. He was a sensualist, who loved witty conversation, champagne suppers, art, music, and wild rides into Paris for a night at the theater. Marie preferred sedate

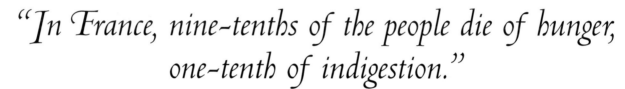

"In France, nine-tenths of the people die of hunger, one-tenth of indigestion."

Tensions with Spain seemed a small price to pay for a secure succession to the throne.

The wedding took place on September 5, 1725, at the palace of Fontainebleau, 35 miles south of Paris. Whatever the bride lacked in personal glamour, she made up for in the magnificence of her attire. She wore a diamond crown on her head, a cape and skirt of lush purple velvet trimmed with ermine, a bodice ablaze with a rainbow of precious gems. In the quantity and size of his jewels, though, Louis virtually outshone his bride. Small diamonds sparkled among the golden threads of his brocade wedding suit; another single—and enormous—diamond flashed upon his white-plumed hat.

After a public wedding feast and a magnificent fireworks display, the newlyweds retired to the State Bedchamber. Wakeful courtiers entertained themselves with speculations about events

evenings at home among a circle of companions who were elderly in manner if not in years. The rapier-like cut and thrust of courtly conversation was not to her taste. She liked idle chat and simple card games, varied by a little enthusiastic twanging and tootling on various musical instruments. No one could fault her many acts of charity or her amiable nature, but even her fond father had once admitted, "When I'm with her I yawn as if at Mass."

The royal pair seemed to live on two entirely different planets. By the late 1730s their physical relationship was over. The queen, worn out by years of almost continuous pregnancies, childbirths, and miscarriages, had grown increasingly reluctant to welcome Louis to her bed. Louis took these developments with a philosophical shrug; indeed, his own ardor for Marie had long since cooled.

Marital fidelity was not a virtue expected of French kings,

and royal mistresses were a familiar fixture at court. Still, Louis was initially discreet in his extramarital adventurings, neither wishing nor needing to stray beyond his intimate circle. His first mistresses, in fact, were all sisters from the same noble family, the Mailly-Nesles; for a time, two of them—Louise, the comtesse de Mailly, and her younger sibling Félicité—amicably shared the royal attentions. Another, more jealous sister described Félicité as having "the figure of a grenadier, the neck of a crane, and the smell of a monkey." When Félicité, pregnant, retired from the fray, the king married her off to a suitable noble.

A third sister, Adélaïde, also was no beauty. She was, however, witty, and specialized in mimicking her fellow courtiers. The king liked people who could make him laugh; he duly bestowed his favors. But Adélaïde soon found herself upstaged by an equally clever and far more beautiful sister, Marie-Anne. This charming and ambitious usurper refused to share her place in the sun with anybody—even her own flesh and blood. Louis, thoroughly smitten, yielded to her demands for exclusivity and rewarded her with the lucrative duchy of Châteauroux.

Once he had successfully produced an heir and organized his love life to his own apparent satisfaction, Louis threw himself into his other favorite pastimes with fresh vigor. At Versailles he spent his off-duty hours carving ivory in a little workshop in his private apartments or paying surprise visits to the courtiers he liked best. He was even known to walk along the rooftops of the palace, entering by a window—or, on one occasion, via the chimney—into the apartments of friends.

When he wished an even more dramatic break from courtly decorum, Louis organized hunting parties. His favorite resort was the little château of Choisy, a newly acquired lodge in the Forest of Sénart, along the Seine just south of Paris. To this leafy retreat Louis brought small groups of his most convivial male and female friends. Dress and manners were informal. The ladies walked about in simple, comfortable gowns that would have raised eyebrows among the stiffly garbed style setters back at Versailles, and the king himself made the coffee. To enhance the relaxed atmosphere, meals were delivered from kitchen to dining room by an ingenious mechanical dumbwaiter, allowing the company the rare opportunity to enjoy themselves out of sight and earshot of the servants.

The respites at Choisy also gave the king a chance to savor the pleasures of life in the open air. Sometimes he would spend entire days sitting on the riverbank, conversing with the boatmen whose barges ferried wine and fish into Paris. Louis charmed them by his easy sociability and his obvious interest in their lives and work. This lapse from the traditional royal remoteness did his reputation no harm among the populace.

But no recreation gave him greater joy than a hard day on the hunting grounds. Unlike many aficionados of the chase, Louis took scrupulous care to protect the local farmers' fields from damage. Any companion who carelessly trampled a crop would never be invited to join the royal hunt again. Courtiers vied with one another for the privilege of riding with His Majesty—according to protocol, only aristocrats from the oldest families in France had the right to share his sport.

As a courtesy, the king bent the rules just enough to allow the local elite to follow the hunt as spectators. Grateful, they kept their carriages at a respectful distance. But one daring individual repeatedly flouted this convention. Like a beribboned and petticoated Diana, goddess of the hunt, she whipped her horses along the forest tracks, always managing to emerge, seemingly accidentally, from the greenery right before the eyes of the king.

Louis, intrigued, made inquiries. Madame d'Étioles was the wife of a gentleman resident in the vicinity, but there was nothing matronly about the looks she flashed him from her gaily painted carriage. No conversation passed between them, but he found out where she lived and began sending little gift parcels of the game bagged at his hunts.

It didn't take long for the king's current mistress, the duchesse de Châteauroux, to learn that there was a poacher at large in the Forest of Sénart. So she made sure that a message winged its way to the lovely Madame d'Étioles, suggesting that it would be a good idea for her to abandon her little carriage drives. Madame d'Étioles prudently decided to exercise her horses elsewhere. But she bided her time.

Meanwhile the king was free to hunt and otherwise enjoy life, secure in the knowledge that his realm remained in safe hands—those of Cardinal André-Hercule de Fleury, his most trusted minister. Fleury had been appointed royal tutor in 1715 and had made good use of his position at the heart of Versailles to become wise in the ways of statecraft. Even the philosopher Voltaire, who viewed most churchmen with a jaundiced eye, thought highly of the cardinal: "He never made a merit of his own services, nor complained of others, and never engaged in cabals or intrigues of the court."

The "circumspection of his conduct and the amiability of his disposition" that so impressed Voltaire contrasted markedly with the style of his predecessor and enemy, the power-hungry and conspiratorial duc de Bourbon. In 1726, when the duke had tried to have Fleury dismissed, the 16-year-old king had sided with his tutor. No one had been more stunned than Monsieur le Duc when Louis, after smilingly bestowing gifts and urging him to come to dinner, had suddenly handed the duke a letter relieving him of his position as chief minister and removing him from court.

Monsieur le Duc was luckier than some recipients of the dreaded royal document known as a *lettre de cachet,* which could imprison a man in the Bastille at the king's pleasure, without the hindrance of a trial. The duke's punishment had been less draconian: banishment to his own castle of Chantilly. His mistress, Madame de Prie, also found herself sent away; unfortunately, the king wished her to retire to her estate in Normandy, far enough from Monsieur le Duc to prevent them from continuing their intrigues. Devastated, the marquise who had brokered the royal marriage ended her own life with a dose of poison.

No matter which faction he or she belonged to, every courtier at Versailles could sympathize with Madame de Prie's despair. Exile from the royal presence was dreaded as a fate worse than death. The upper echelons of the French nobility literally lived at Versailles, either within the sprawling palace or in the immediate vicinity.

This intimate ingathering of the ruling class had been engineered as a deliberate policy in the previous reign. Louis XIV, fearful of an upper-class revolt, sent out a corps of centrally appointed bureaucrats, called intendants, to govern the provinces previously con-

Astride the white mount at the center of this hunting scene, Louis XV exhorts his dogs to close in on a trapped stag. Robust and athletic, the king hunted for several hours each day, exhausting hounds, horses, and fellow huntsmen alike.

trolled by the great nobles. In exchange, these nobles were enticed to join the glittering cavalcade of life in the aura of the Sun King. Power and influence no longer emerged from the provinces but now were dispersed from the corridors of Versailles.

By the time Louis XV came to the throne, the members of this inward-looking community referred to themselves and their surroundings as *ce pays-ci*—literally, "this country." It was, indeed, an exotic land, with its own complex rules and mysterious rituals, played out against the elegant—but often physically uncomfortable—backdrop of milelong corridors, gold-embroidered tapestries, lush velvet cushions, and marble floors.

Under a lady's silken sleeve or a gentleman's brocade, elbows were sharp. Courtiers fought fiercely, desperate to sidle near enough to the king to gain his attention. There was no other route to promotion, no other way to beg a favor. And no one was allowed to forget whatever degree of status they had achieved, through blood or shrewd maneuvering: At court the right to sit on a chair as opposed to a stool, or even the freedom to sit down at all, was entirely dependent on rank.

During the reign of Louis XV, though, foreign wars, an anemic domestic economy, and the ruling class's own profligacy took their toll. The aristocracy was unable to indulge itself quite as extravagantly as it had during the previous reign. Even so exalted a figure as a royal mistress might feel the pinch. The comtesse de

Mailly, the king's first paramour from the Mailly-Nesle family, found it impossible to pay even modest gambling debts. She was "poorer than ever," sneered one nobleman. "Her chemises are worn out and full of holes, and her lady's maid badly dressed, which is a sign of true poverty."

Nobility itself was becoming a commodity subject to devaluation. The old landowning aristocrats, descendants of feudal barons, found themselves jostled by newer titleholders drawn from the ranks of wealthy commoners—purchasers of official positions that conferred nobility.

Cardinal Fleury, presiding over these changing times, tried to ease the pressure on the realm by introducing a number of reforms. Although he was in his 70s when he came to power—and a member of the conservative church hierarchy—Fleury's views were far more progressive than those of his predecessor. He eased the rigid censorship laws instituted by Monsieur le Duc and freed the political dissidents that the duke had jailed in the Bastille. He also attempted to balance the budget, cutting superfluous government expenditure.

A large part of the state's revenues came from taxes on consumer goods. Instead of cranking up the tax rate even higher—and alienating an already hard-pressed populace—he tried to increase the volume of trade, improving the roads and increasing the number of cargo vessels.

Despite the cardinal's reforms, the vast majority of Louis's subjects still saw around half their earnings sucked away by the taxgatherers. Direct taxes of various kinds were supplemented by a legion of indirect taxes—taxes on salt, iron, leather, wine, soap, tobacco, and playing cards, to name but a

Seen here in his cardinal's robes, chief minister André-Hercule de Fleury virtually ruled France from 1726 to 1743. An able and gracious administrator, he stabilized the economy by curbing inflation and expanding trade.

few. To taxes owed the king were added those demanded by the clergy and nobility. It did not escape the notice of urban artisans and rural peasants that they were the ones who did most of the paying. Nobles and the clergy, by ancient right or underassessment, enjoyed exemption from some direct taxes and escaped the full weight of others. Those who could least afford the taxes were those who carried the burden. Even the Neapolitan ambassador was taken aback by the yawning gulf between the opulent lifestyle of the aristocracy and the penury of the lower classes. "In France," he noted, "nine-tenths of the people die of hunger, one-tenth of indigestion."

There was, indeed, resentment on the streets and in the coffeehouses of Paris, directed both at Louis and at his chief minister. "O king born to hunt deer," asked one poetic dissident, "will you always be the slave of an octogenarian prelate?" Fleury was, after all, not just a politician but a prince of the church, and his reforming zeal did not extend to matters of religion. France was in the throes of a prolonged theological war between religious conservatives and the unorthodox Jansenists. These dissenters dared to suggest that spiritual truth, far from being the sole preserve of popes and bishops, was accessible to individual Catholics.

Jansenism had gained widespread support among lawyers, merchants, and artisans, as well as many ordinary parish priests; its opponents included such prominent members of the ruling class as the ultrapious queen and the dauphin, heir to the throne. Meanwhile, from the sidelines, a new breed of philosophical freethinkers, led by Voltaire, dared to scoff at both sets of believers. Yet religious diversity was hardly the order of the day: Protestantism remained against the law, and those who flouted the ban still faced persecution—imprisonment, servitude in the galleys, confiscation of property, or the forcible removal of their children to Catholic homes.

To defend pontifical authority, the pope had issued a bull, or decree, condemning 101 points of Jansenist doctrine. Many Jansenist clerics refused to accept it. In 1730 Cardinal Fleury persuaded the king to enact a law forbidding any dying person from receiving the last rites unless they had made their confession to a priest who accepted the terms of the bull. The new legislation did little to help relations between Louis and the Jansenists, who dominated the parlement in Paris.

In arenas where the authority of the church was not at stake, Fleury much preferred peace to war. He struggled to keep the king from embroiling France in the dynastic conflicts that were tearing Europe apart. But in 1741 a faction of militaristic nobles—led, it was alleged, by the Mailly-Nesle sister reigning as royal mistress at the time—persuaded Louis to join Frederick the Great of Prussia's campaign against the young empress Maria Theresa of Austria. Frederick's avowed intention was to challenge her claim to the Austrian throne. The hidden agenda, for both Prussia and France, was the chance to carve up the Austrian empire between themselves if they won. The conflict, called the War of the Austrian Succession, punctuated by occasional lulls in the fighting, short-lived treaties, and periodic double-dealing among the allies, dragged on for seven more years. Fleury, opposed to the war and embittered by the young king's refusal to listen to his wisdom, gave up his ministerial post and went home to his château at Issy, where he died at age 90, in 1743.

Louis, now 33 years old, decided that, after 20 years of kingship, he felt qualified to rule without a mentor. He announced that Fleury would not be replaced; His Majesty would act as his own chief minister. His confidence high, he sallied forth to the war zone. The duchesse de Châteauroux, girding herself like a less saintly Joan of Arc, followed him to the front.

At the army's headquarters in Metz, Louis came down with fever. Days of relentless bloodletting, alternating with purges as fierce as cannon fire, only seemed to make matters worse. His status-conscious entourage squabbled over rights of access to the sickroom. And everyone speculated in excited whispers: If the king believed himself near death, he would, for the sake of his immortal soul, have to repent his adultery and break with his mistress before receiving the last rites. Those loyal to the duchess, and dependent on her patronage, dreaded this possibility as much as she did. Another faction devoutly hoped for her dismissal.

In the end the church prevailed. At the royal bedside, the bishop of Soissons persuaded Louis to banish the duchess and to make a full confession of his sins. The bishop saw to it that every word was recorded and the text circulated throughout the realm. In spite of the doctors' attempts to drain most of the blood from his body, however, the king recovered. The nation rejoiced. They hailed their sovereign with a new sobriquet: "Louis the Beloved."

Louis's own relief was mingled with

satisfaction of diplomats and the public's delight, the king's oldest son, the dauphin, had just married a Spanish princess; the gathering at Versailles was one of the high points of the month-long wedding celebrations.

Although the young bridegroom disliked balls, his father couldn't get enough of them. Balls held in the State Apartments were open to all comers, as long as they came dressed with suitable magnificence. To avoid being mobbed by his adoring public, Louis adopted a clever ruse. He and seven male courtiers came costumed as eight identical yew trees, clipped in the topiary style favored by the palace gardeners.

Thanks to his leafy disguise, Louis passed undisturbed through a half-dozen crowded reception rooms, each of which had

"*If there has to be a mistress, better this one than any other.*"

anger. He was mortified by the publication of his confession. If there was anything he truly repented now, it was his surrender to the bishop over the matter of Madame de Châteauroux. His official reconciliation with the queen upon his return to Versailles was an empty formality. When he tried to visit, she ignored his scratching—the court's version of a knock—at her bedroom door. Nor was there any hope of reunion with his mistress: In December 1744, four months after her exile, the duchesse de Châteauroux died of pneumonia.

On a February evening, barely two months after the death of Madame de Châteauroux, King Louis's valets completed the intricate task of disguising their royal master as a tree. The occasion was a costume ball, the largest and most spectacular entertainment in the sparkling history of revelry at Versailles. To the

its own buffet and band. Here, bejeweled commoners did battle with princesses dressed as flower sellers over the sumptuous buffet tables, jostling for the choicest morsel of salmon and the biggest slab of trout pâté. As purposeful as a cat sniffing mice, the king made his way to the Hall of Mirrors. There he found his quarry, and he pounced.

The lady in question masqueraded in the garb of Diana, goddess of the hunt. Louis may well have smiled at her choice of apparel, for she was the selfsame Madame d'Étioles who had distracted him so prettily from his hunts in the Forest of Sénart. Engrossed in conversation, both took off their masks; the chemistry between them did not go unnoticed.

The court was appalled, but titillated. Royal mistresses, with their unparalleled access to the king, could exercise considerable power within the realm. It was customary, and most comfortable for the court, for them to belong to the class that had been born to rule. Unlike her predecessors, however, this new favorite came not from the old landed nobility but from the Parisian bourgeoisie: Her father was an undistinguished businessman surnamed Poisson—literally, Fish.

Young Jeanne-Antoinette, though, had always known herself destined for greater things. She was bright, pretty rather than beautiful, warm and enthusiastic, witty, artistic, kindhearted, and blessed with considerable charm. And she never forgot what a fortuneteller had predicted for her, at the tender age of nine: "that I would be the King's mistress." She'd made no secret of this prophecy, and her family, amused rather than scandalized, henceforth nicknamed her Reinette, "Little Queen."

When her financier father's business collapsed, young Reinette and her family had been rescued from penury by a discreet donation from her mother's wealthy lover, Monsieur Le Normant de Tournehem—ex-ambassador to Sweden and a far more prudent speculator than Monsieur Poisson. Tournehem had also helped broker Reinette's marriage to his nephew. Monsieur d'Étioles proved a devoted husband, delighted when she bore him a daughter. But when the king's shadow fell across his marriage bed, d'Étioles grudgingly surrendered to the inevitable.

Louis knew that there would be plenty of hostile eyes at court, watching keenly to catch his new beloved in some gross social error. Sensitive to the gulf between his 24-year-old mis-

tress and the aristocratic denizens of Versailles, the king prevailed upon a couple of trusted courtiers to take Madame d'Étioles away to her own country house near Choisy for an intensive course in the arcane etiquette of ce pays-ci.

To celebrate their separateness, the denizens of ce pays-ci had evolved their own private language. The newcomer would find herself a laughingstock if, like millions of the king's subjects, she spoke of her house as *chez moi* instead of the courtiers' *chev moi* or pronounced the final *c* in *sac*—at Versailles a bag was a *sa*. Heaven help her if she walked with an ordinary stride: Court

ladies had to perfect a strange gliding maneuver. Nobles of different ranks merited curtsies of varying depths and angles.

To make sure she knew exactly which people deserved which perquisites, Madame d'Étioles's tutors toured her through the family trees of the most important noble houses. With exquisite tact, they briefed her on the long-running feuds that seethed behind the charming chatter and compulsory smiles of the royal entourage. Then, holding their breath, they watched their pupil set sail upon the dangerous waters of Versailles.

By the time she arrived at court she was no longer Madame d'Étioles. The king had elevated her to the nobility, transforming her into the marquise de Pompadour. Along with the title came estates and a coat of arms: three castles on an azure field. Her new status also entailed a rite of passage, a formal presentation at court. Custom required her to make an inaugural bow not only to His Majesty but to the queen. It promised to be the most dramatic debut of the century. No courtier worth the powder on his wig would have dreamed of missing it.

On the afternoon of her debut, Madame de Pompadour's new apartments at Versailles resembled a military headquarters. The occupants of the marquise's perfumed boudoir were as purposeful as Louis's generals planning tactics on the Austrian front. Maids bustled about, carrying lace, silks, dazzling white linen, rustling taffeta, embroidered satin, velvets so lush they glowed like ripe fruits. Close friends, invited to watch the preparations, helped ease the tense atmosphere with idle chatter.

The lady herself sat at her dressing table surrounded by the weapons assembled for the coming battle. From onyx jars, lapis lazuli boxes, and golden compacts came creams, rouge, paints,

Madame de Pompadour was Louis's mistress for less than a decade, but they remained friends for the rest of her life. In this portrait by François Boucher, both stages of their relationship are suggested by the sculpture behind Pompadour, *Love and Friendship.*

and powders. She contemplated her stockpile of beauty marks—black silk patches in the shape of teardrops, hearts, stars, crescent moons. She selected half a dozen of these tiny ornaments to paste onto her cheeks, her forehead, and anywhere else they might draw attention to a dimple or add a grace note to a smile.

With the gravity of a squire helping a knight into his armor, a maid assisted Pompadour into the undergarment deemed essential by every woman of fashion—the pannier, or hoop skirt. This construction was so wide that its wearer sometimes had to pass through a door sideways and—at the theater—required two or even three chairs to accommodate it. Prudish priests lambasted the pannier wearers as "she-monkeys" and "clerks of the devil"; the objects of their attacks simply swung their hoops around and walked away. Panniers gave a lady, whatever her shape, a certain mystery and grandeur; unfortunately, they also kept her at a distance from her closest confidantes, hindering intimate exchanges. "I could not whisper to Madame d'Egmont," one noblewoman complained, "because our hoops prevented our being near together."

Gowned in opulently embroidered satin, with a little headdress of white feathers and diamonds on her powdered hair, Madame de Pompadour sallied forth with her entourage. The courtier in charge of making the formal presentation was the elderly but raffish princess de Conti, a cousin of the king; she'd taken on the assignment in order to curry favor with Louis, hoping he would bail her out of her prodigious gambling debts.

The silken sea of courtiers parted, scrutinizing Pompadour's well-rehearsed glide through the state rooms and into the council chamber. Here, with no visible sign of irony, the newly ennobled marquise de Pompadour made her ritual triple curtsy to a blushing Louis; the man whose bedclothes still smelled of her perfume mumbled an acknowledgment and quickly turned away as Pompadour backed—without a misstep—out of the royal presence.

Next came the moment everyone was waiting for: Pompadour's presentation to Marie Leszczyńska. All Versailles, having speculated enthusiastically over the likelihood of a queenly snub, held its breath as the princess de Conti ushered her charge into the queen's salon. The cognoscenti had predicted that Her Majesty would pay her rival a bland compliment on her gown and then say nothing more; in the esoteric code of ce pays-ci such a brief exchange would be the equivalent of a slap in the face. But the queen stunned everybody. She saluted Pompadour in a cordial manner, then launched into a little chat about a mutual acquaintance. Pompadour, almost babbling with relief, declared her devotion to the queen and vowed to serve her to the best of her ability. The cognoscenti, ears flapping, monitored both the content and duration of this exchange: Her Majesty had spoken a full 12 sentences to her husband's paramour. This was the world turned upside down.

The queen, as it happened, was breathing her own quiet sigh of relief. Previous royal mistresses, especially the comtesse de Mailly, had treated her callously and taken every opportunity to demean her in the king's eyes. Marie Leszczyńska could see at once that this little bourgeoise was infinitely kinder and more sensitive than her aristocratic predecessors. No native of ce pays-ci would ever have displayed such warmth or expressed her emotions so openly. "If there has to be a mistress," said the queen to her intimates, "better this one than any other."

Pompadour still had one more ordeal to endure before the night was over—formal presentation to the dauphin. The heir to the throne, unforgiving of his father's adultery, received the marquise as brusquely as the most malicious courtier could wish. According to some onlookers, he stuck out his tongue as she left his apartment. And, for years thereafter, he spoke of her only as "Madame Whore."

With this trial by curtsy over, the marquise settled into her new life. Louis, however smitten, had a realm to rule, so she had plenty of time to pursue her own interests. She gathered stimu-

Pompadour had thousands of scented china flowers, like those shown here, planted in the grounds of her Bellevue château southwest of Paris. Although she owned many homes, Bellevue—depicted at left in a painting that decorates a snuffbox—was the only residence that the marquise had built for herself.

lating friends about her, wrote witty letters, and indulged her passion for gardening, collecting exotic scented plants from all over the world. Unlike most of her fellow courtiers, she was an unabashed intellectual. Her library contained some 3,500 volumes, reflecting her eclectic tastes. She enjoyed Perrault's collection of French fairy tales, translations of *Tom Jones* and *Robinson Crusoe,* history, philosophy, the essays of Voltaire, as well as medieval romances and the true-crime sagas detailed in the police reports.

Long before her arrival at court, Madame de Pompadour had befriended many prominent figures of the French Enlightenment—Voltaire himself, the *encyclopédistes* Diderot and d'Alembert, the philosopher Rousseau. The king himself never shared her literary enthusiasms. But she was able to use her influence to provide Voltaire with a court post and a pension and to intervene on behalf of radical thinkers who fell afoul of the censors or the church.

To assure herself of a constant source of intellectual stimulation, she recruited the

SÈVRES PORCELAIN

In 1756 Madame de Pompadour moved French china production from Vincennes, east of Paris, to Sèvres, closer to the court at Versailles and to her new home at Bellevue. Under royal patronage, Sèvres porcelain grew to rival the wares of China and Meissen in Saxony. The Sèvres inkstand shown above probably belonged to Louis XV's daughter Madame Adélaïde. The terrestrial globe *(right)* served as an inkwell, the celestial globe held sand to dry the ink, and the crown housed a bell for calling servants.

surgeon and economic reformer François Quesnay as her personal physician. He was installed in an apartment below her own. In her free hours she liked to slip down and join Quesnay and his philosophically minded visitors in discussing the issues of the day.

Taking advantage of her newfound wealth and position, Pompadour became an enthusiastic patron of the visual arts. Her many protégés included François Boucher, who painted her portrait as she sat at her dressing table, putting the finishing touches to her toilette. She reveled in the fashionable rococo style with its playful curves and arabesques, its Arcadian landscapes, rosy goddesses, and pastel hues.

Her annual household expenses averaged 33,000 livres; it was later estimated she spent more than 36 million livres in her lifetime. Pompadour's expensive tastes, jeered her critics, made her a bigger drain on the exchequer than a foreign war. But she gladdened the hearts and made the fortunes of France's jewelers, cabinetmakers, glassblowers, silversmiths, and architects.

She refurbished royal residences and constructed new hideaways—a magnificent château at Bellevue, quaint follies at Versailles, Fontainebleau, and Compiègne—for her intimate moments with the king. He liked to dress in his hunting clothes, loudly trumpet that he was off in pursuit of game, and then slip away to one of these hermitages to enjoy a cozy afternoon with the marquise.

Ever inventive, Pompadour also devised a new amusement that delighted both the king and his closest circle of friends. She designed a tiny theater, seating only 14, with painted decorations by Boucher, and recruited an elite band of talented courtiers, who were drilled as rigorously as professional actors. The company made its debut on January 17, 1747, in a production of *Le Tartuffe* by Molière. The king, whose attendance at the official court theater had often been inspired by duty rather than passion, found these amateur theatricals far more entertaining, especially since his mistress took most of the starring roles. The competition to join His Majesty in this private little playhouse was fierce; Pompadour enjoyed her power to close the door on those who displeased her.

But the patter of royal applause in the Théâtre des Petits Cabinets could not drown out the attacks on Pompadour emanating from her enemies at court. Members of the conservative, ultra-religious faction known as the Dévots loathed Pompadour for her friendship with notorious freethinkers as well as for her sinful liaison with the king. Senior ministers and those ambitious for high office resented her sway over Louis. When, in 1752, he made her a duchess, their blood boiled.

This loathing poured out of Versailles like a toxic flood. In the palace and in Paris, scandalmongers had a field day. Court wags circulated a little series of verses called *Poissonades,* reveling in Pompadour's unromantic maiden name. Some of these efforts were downright obscene; others mocked her bourgeois origins: "If the Court is vulgar / why should that surprise us? / Isn't it from the market that Fish comes to us?" It was even whispered that, when she couldn't satisfy Louis's sexual appetites herself, she acted as his procuress.

An increasingly hungry and hard-pressed populace, hearing tales of Pompadour's excesses, grew ever more disenchanted. But courtiers glad to see the royal mistress lampooned in the taverns of Paris soon found that the resentful public made no distinction between her extravagance and that of anyone else at Versailles. The romance between the king and his subjects, so warm in the days of his illness at Metz, had cooled considerably. No one called Louis "the Beloved" anymore. The War of the Austrian Succession had ended in a disappointing treaty, with few advantages for France, making even his loyal subjects wonder what all those years of conflict, all that expenditure of men and money, had been about. King and mistress prudently stayed out of the capital. Pompadour, however, acquired an additional set of eyes and ears in the person of her protégé Nicolas-René Berryer, head of the

EARLY FRENCH HAUTE COUTURE

France during the 18th century was the undisputed leader of world fashion. At Versailles, nobles vied with one another to wear the latest styles: coiffures so high that while riding in carriages, women were forced to kneel or to travel with their heads pointing out the window; towering head-dresses that, according to one critic, "made a woman's face look as if it was in the middle of her body" *(right)*; and skirts so wide that short women looked like balls, tall women looked like bells, and staircases actually had to be redesigned in order to accommodate them.

"The foolish set the fashions," one commentator wrote despairingly. But where the foolish led, the wealthy followed. In an effort to emulate the styles at Versailles, outsiders at first relied on wooden dolls known as Pandoras, which were dressed in the most recent court fashions and sent to Paris and other cities to be copied. As printing techniques developed, however, journals began to feature fashion drawings, or plates, offering details of the styles worn by the nobility. Now any woman with the inclination—and the money—could visit one of Paris's 1,700 dressmaking shops and look like the grand ladies at court.

Le triomphe du ridicule

The most famous Paris dressmaker was Rose Bertin *(above)*, whose reputation was made when future queen Marie-Antoinette ordered from her.

Marie-Antoinette set many of the styles at court. "When the Queen passed along the gallery at Versailles," noted an observer, "you could see nothing but a forest of feathers, rising a foot and a half above the head, and nodding to and fro."

In this caricature from a 1773 almanac, birds attack a woman sporting a headpiece surrounded by a huge array of feathers.

Among the most outlandish headdresses at court were those representing mountains, forests, and *(below)* a French warship.

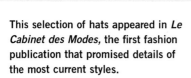

This selection of hats appeared in *Le Cabinet des Modes,* the first fashion publication that promised details of the most current styles.

Paris police, who ran a network of informers and made sure that anyone who criticized either His Majesty or the marquise found themselves in prison.

However cool and poised she might appear at court soirees, however energetic in her intellectual and artistic endeavors, Pompadour began to suffer from the stresses of her extraordinary life. In a desperate attempt to keep pace with Louis's prodigious sexual energies, she ate crayfish, vanilla, and other supposedly aphrodisiac foods until she became nauseated. Her health suffered; she had miscarriages and sometimes spit blood. In 1754 the death of her only child, her 10-year-old daughter, Alexandrine d'Étioles—probably from a case of appendicitis—sent her into a deep depression. By the following year her sexual relationship with the king was over.

Yet Pompadour's influence over Louis grew even as their passion waned. He'd long respected her judgment on domestic affairs and appointed her favorites to key positions. Now she began to play a conspicuous role in foreign policy too. And it did not escape her critics' notice that, when speaking of the king's deliberations, she included herself in the royal "We."

In 1756 France found itself at war on

two continents. Once again, Europe was in turmoil, with former allies now at loggerheads and old enemies coming together. France and Austria joined forces to stop Prussian expansion; the prolonged struggle became known as the Seven Years' War. Meanwhile, on the other side of the Atlantic, France and Britain battled for control of North America; the conflict, later named the French and Indian War, would also drag on until 1763. Neither ended in victory for France.

While Louis's soldiers grappled with the enemy, their noble commanders often seemed more interested in fighting each other, transferring the old factional hatreds from Versailles to the front. It was said that at least one crucial battle was lost when the prince de Soubise, a general appointed by Pompadour, failed to receive desperately needed reinforcements because the duc de Richelieu—who detested the lady—refused to send them until it was too late. The defeat, at Rossbach in Saxony, was perhaps the most shameful ever suffered by the French forces.

Back at court, the anti-Pompadour contingent mocked Soubise's defeat with a crop of malicious jingles and lampoons. Pompadour, perceiving this catastrophe as a turning point in their fortunes and feeling an overwhelming sense of impending doom, reportedly said to Louis, "After us, the deluge." The phrase would have good cause to be remembered; it was more prophetic than she knew.

When the conflicts ended, Louis's overseas empire was in tatters. Another Pompadour protégé, minister of foreign affairs Étienne-François Choiseul, negotiated the Treaty of Paris that concluded the colonial war. Although forced to cede Canada, the vast Louisiana territory, and most of the country's holdings in India, Choiseul managed to ensure that France's rich sugar islands in the West Indies stayed under French control. In an effort to prevent any further military defeats, he reformed the army and expanded the French fleet.

Madame de Pompadour's friends among the philosophes,

especially Voltaire, celebrated when Choiseul and his allies ended the Jesuits' stranglehold over education and drove the order out of France. But Pompadour herself had other preoccupations: She was only 42, but her health, never robust, was finally failing. The cold winter of 1764 dragged on into a foul and miserable travesty of a spring. Struggling to draw the chilly air into her incurably congested lungs, Pompadour accepted the inevitable. She made her will and, at the king's urging, summoned a priest to hear her confession and administer the last rites.

She had been reluctant to do so, however. Once she had formally repented their 20-year liaison, Louis could no longer remain at her side. Ever scrupulous about protocol, he bade her farewell and walked out of her chamber. When she drew her last breath, on Palm Sunday of 1764, her old friends Soubise and Choiseul were in attendance. The king was in church, safe from any awkward interruption.

Protocol forbade the presence of any dead body, apart from a royal corpse, within the palace. Terrified of breaching this taboo, Pompadour's servants refused to wait until her coach could be made ready. They placed her sheeted body on a stretcher and carried her out the gates of Versailles. She would be buried two days later, in the Paris church that housed the tomb of her young daughter, Alexandrine.

Protocol also forbade the king to attend the funeral. But he watched from a balcony as Pompadour's cortege moved through the battering wind and freezing rain. He was devastated, but he knew better than to display his grief before the sharp-eyed denizens of ce pays-ci. A few days later the queen—bemused at surviving her most tenacious rival—wrote to a friend: "Nobody talks here of *what is no more,* it is as if she had never existed."

On July 27, 1774, the highest nobles of France assembled at the ancient abbey church of Saint-Denis to pay their final respects to Louis XV. The funeral rites would last a full five hours, and even the most devout among the mourners could hardly keep their minds from wandering. They mulled over the ghastly drama of the old king's last days.

At a quarter past three on the afternoon of May 10, the single candle flickering in the window of the royal apartments had been extinguished, signifying that the deathwatch had finally come to an end. As the flame disappeared, the entire court—including the new monarch, Louis XVI, and his queen, Marie-Antoinette—had flung themselves into carriages, ordered their coachmen to whip the horses hard, and sped away from Versailles.

The specter that drove them off in such terror was smallpox. The disease, which had turned the king into a mass of foul-smelling, rotting sores, was as rampant as it was infectious. It afflicted 95 percent of the French population, killing one out of every seven victims. Louis's corpse, encased in two lead caskets, had been conveyed by night to Saint-Denis and quickly sealed into the royal crypt. The official funeral—delayed until those courtiers exposed to the dying king emerged from quarantine—took place over an empty coffin.

Louis XV had occupied the throne for 60 years; most of his subjects had no memory of any other king. To mark his passing, everyone from the loftiest prince to the lowliest fishwife draped themselves in

Louis XVI (right) may have lacked the will and charisma of his grandfather, Louis XV, yet he sincerely tried to implement reforms. For a nation impatient for change, it was too little, too late. The political naiveté of his Austrian-born queen, Marie-Antoinette—shown above with their children—cemented opposition against them.

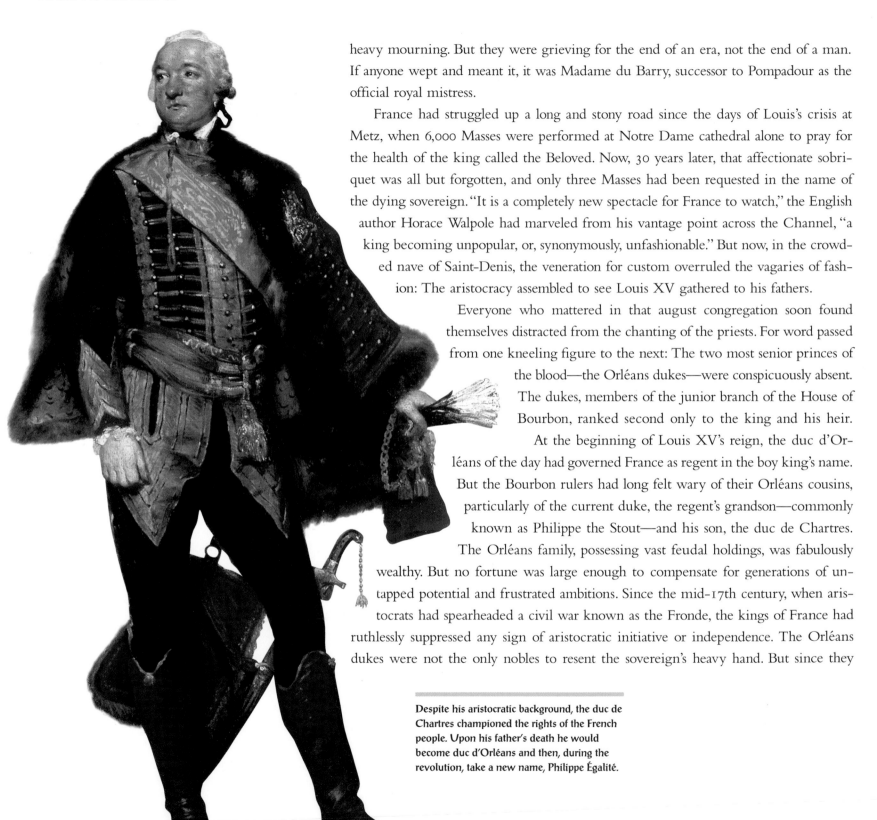

heavy mourning. But they were grieving for the end of an era, not the end of a man. If anyone wept and meant it, it was Madame du Barry, successor to Pompadour as the official royal mistress.

France had struggled up a long and stony road since the days of Louis's crisis at Metz, when 6,000 Masses were performed at Notre Dame cathedral alone to pray for the health of the king called the Beloved. Now, 30 years later, that affectionate sobriquet was all but forgotten, and only three Masses had been requested in the name of the dying sovereign. "It is a completely new spectacle for France to watch," the English author Horace Walpole had marveled from his vantage point across the Channel, "a king becoming unpopular, or, synonymously, unfashionable." But now, in the crowded nave of Saint-Denis, the veneration for custom overruled the vagaries of fashion: The aristocracy assembled to see Louis XV gathered to his fathers.

Everyone who mattered in that august congregation soon found themselves distracted from the chanting of the priests. For word passed from one kneeling figure to the next: The two most senior princes of the blood—the Orléans dukes—were conspicuously absent. The dukes, members of the junior branch of the House of Bourbon, ranked second only to the king and his heir.

At the beginning of Louis XV's reign, the duc d'Orléans of the day had governed France as regent in the boy king's name. But the Bourbon rulers had long felt wary of their Orléans cousins, particularly of the current duke, the regent's grandson—commonly known as Philippe the Stout—and his son, the duc de Chartres. The Orléans family, possessing vast feudal holdings, was fabulously wealthy. But no fortune was large enough to compensate for generations of untapped potential and frustrated ambitions. Since the mid-17th century, when aristocrats had spearheaded a civil war known as the Fronde, the kings of France had ruthlessly suppressed any sign of aristocratic initiative or independence. The Orléans dukes were not the only nobles to resent the sovereign's heavy hand. But since they

Despite his aristocratic background, the duc de Chartres championed the rights of the French people. Upon his father's death he would become duc d'Orléans and then, during the revolution, take a new name, Philippe Égalité.

stood in line to the throne, they were the ones most likely to trouble his dreams.

Another possible challenge to the monarch's power came from the parlements, the royal courts of law. These bodies, located in Paris and various provincial centers, were courts of appeal responsible for upholding the law and giving judicial effect to the king's edicts. But their members—aristocratic magistrates from ancient and more recently ennobled families who had purchased their seats in the parlement—had an ancient right. If a law proposed by the king seemed to them to be inconsistent with existing law or judicial precedent, they could protest and refuse to inscribe it into the statute books.

Throughout the 1750s and 1760s the Parlement of Paris, supported by other parlements in the provinces, had clashed with

old king was dead, Chartres made it clear that he would carry his fight into the reign of Louis's grandson and successor (the dauphin having died of consumption in 1765). His decision to stay away from the funeral was the opening salvo in that campaign. The irate Louis XVI promptly sent both Chartres and the duke's father into temporary exile at their country estates at Villers-Cotterêts, 40 miles northeast of Paris. But it was not long before he brought back the parlements that had been suppressed by his grandfather.

The old duc d'Orléans, Philippe the Stout, may have been banished along with his son, but it was the younger Philippe, duc de Chartres, who was the real thorn in the new king's side. Chartres was a complicated, often contradictory character. He was a sensualist—his detractors, and they were legion, called him a

"All men are equal. None can stand above another or command him; sovereigns must belong to the multitude."

Louis XV and his ministers over issues of taxation and state finance, economic policy, and the administration of religion. Tensions had become so acute that in 1771 the government suppressed the country's parlements, substituting new courts made up of royal appointees. This action had sparked widespread protests among the elite and angry murmurs in the streets, as well as a storm of pamphlets denouncing royal despotism in tones that were to unleash a revolution a quarter of a century later.

The duc de Chartres had been among those who had sprung to the parlements' defense, condemning their suppression as a move to give Louis XV absolute power. And now, though the

libertine—who liked nothing better than to spend his nights in the Paris brothels. These amorous escapades had been duly recorded by Louis XV's police spies, whose reports back to Versailles had given the late king some titillating reading.

As much as he loved the ladies, Chartres declared that his first devotion was to the very idea of personal freedom. "My taste for liberty," he explained in a memoir, "caused me to circulate among different classes of society in Paris; there, my opinions were changed or strengthened by healthy debate." He was at once an egalitarian and a snob, happy in the company of racetrack jockeys—he adored fast horses—but contemptuous of the nouveaux riches, perceiving them as a growing threat to his own class.

In contrast to the self-absorbed inhabitants of ce pays-ci, Chartres was an outward-looking cosmopolitan. He was a passionate Anglophile, whose cross-Channel friends included both the Prince of Wales, heir to the British throne, and various politicians of reformist bent. He paid frequent visits to England, the land he called "that womb of liberty." But he hated the fact that, as a prince of the blood, he had to beg his sovereign's permission to travel anywhere outside the borders of France.

According to Chartres, his love of liberty drew him to the Masonic order, which had originated in the British Isles during the mid-1600s and spread through Europe and North America. "I became attached to Freemasonry because it offered me a sort of image of equality." Masonic lodges served as fertile breeding grounds for new philosophical and political ideas. Freemasons were committed to religious tolerance, humanitarianism, intellectual progress, and the universal brotherhood of man.

In 1773 Chartres had become Most Serene Grand Master of the Grand Lodge of France, presiding over its esoteric rites. His royal cousin and the hierarchs of the church would have blanched to hear one of the Masonic oaths Chartres swore: "All men are equal. None can stand above another or command him; sovereigns must belong to the multitude. Peoples bestow sovereignty where they please and retract it when they please. Any religion claiming to be the work of God is an absurdity. Omnipotence that calls itself spiritual is an abuse."

His fondness for England notwithstanding, in July 1778 the 31-year-old duc de Chartres found himself in command during a naval battle against the British. Chafing against the almost com-

pulsory idleness of aristocratic life, he had lobbied the king for a commission as lieutenant general of the fleet. His baptism of fire came in a clash with the Royal Navy near the island of Ouessant, just off the Atlantic coast. The entire battle lasted only half an hour; the French, though holding their ground, failed to destroy a single enemy vessel.

Despite the indecisive outcome, Chartres returned to Paris to the gratifying sound of public applause. When he made an appearance at the Opéra, the audience hailed him as the hero of the hour. At Versailles a chillier reception greeted him. Louis XVI had found little cause for congratulations. At least one dispatch from the combat zone suggested that the French fleet might have fared much better without Chartres in command. And the dangerous duke was the last person the king wished to see basking in the warm glow of popular acclaim. He promptly launched an anti-Chartres smear campaign.

Inspired by a few discreet instructions passed down from on high, anonymous writers churned out libels. Versifiers mocked the duke in doggerel for accepting the adulation at the Opéra; his cowardice, they jeered, was the only thing that had prevented a French victory at Ouessant. Chartres was worse than humiliated: Any hope of a naval career now lay in ruins.

Chartres turned his back entirely on Louis and the court. He, after all, possessed a palace of his own: the ancient Orléans family residence, the Palais Royal. Unlike the gilded cage that was Versailles, the Palais Royal lay in the very center of Paris. And since Louis never deigned to set foot in his capital, Chartres now

Within the gardens of his Paris home, the Palais Royal, Chartres built this great commercial complex, including shops, bookstalls, gaming parlors, private clubs, theaters, and cafés.

resolved to make himself king of the city. He came up with a bold plan to transform the colonnaded precincts of the Palais Royal into an enormous urban pleasure park, full of boutiques, gardens, cafés, clubs, bordellos, billiard parlors, exhibitions, puppet theaters, outdoor shows, and all sorts of carnival attractions. There would, he declared, be something for everyone, "a spectacle and strolling garden for all moments and all seasons."

Despite the protests of some of his neighbors—who lamented the "sacrilegious" destruction of the venerable trees in the *palais* gardens—Chartres knew his scheme would win the hearts of the people of Paris. But this wasn't its only merit. It would also bring in hundreds of thousands of livres in rent from the shopkeepers and stall holders, a desperately needed lifeline for the libertine duke, whose profligate habits had brought him to the verge of bankruptcy. Chartres might be heir to the richest dukedom in France, but his creditors were not prepared to wait until the death of the senior Philippe.

At Versailles the king, receiving details of Chartres's new commercial venture, reacted with malicious glee. What could be more contemptible than the sight of an aristocrat "gone into trade"? The duke soon found another way to defy convention. His various amours had not stopped him from marrying the daughter of the wealthy duc de Penthièvre and becoming a devoted father. And now the time had come to consider the education of little Louis-Philippe, his son and heir. Traditionally, young aristocrats received their schooling from male tutors. Chartres shocked the establishment by entrusting the task to a woman.

The lady in question was the comtesse de Genlis. She was a member of the intelligentsia, an accomplished musician, author of several educational treatises, and—incidentally—Chartres's former mistress. Before she could set to work, the duke had to swallow his pride and ask the king's permission. As a prince of the blood, he required royal approval even for the choice of his children's tutor. This time Louis—delighted by the recent birth of his own son and heir—didn't bother to object. Society at large proved less amenable. When the duke turned up at the theater with his son and new governess

The ascent of this "flying globe" from the Tuileries gardens in December 1783 marked the first manned flight of a hydrogen balloon. Ten days earlier a hot-air balloon launched by the pioneering Montgolfier brothers had carried two men on a 20-minute flight and landed safely.

in tow, the audience booed and jeered. By a droll coincidence, the comedy they'd come to see was called *The Learned Ladies.*

Young Louis-Philippe, who would, long after the revolutionary storms subsided, become the last-ever king of France, joined his siblings in Madame de Genlis's program for molding young minds and bodies. She used a set of 115 specially commissioned paintings to teach Greek and Roman history, regaled her charges with tales of medieval chivalry, and set them to weightlifting and rope climbing in an improvised indoor gymnasium. To introduce his children to the philosophical issues of the day, their father invited Voltaire and other luminaries to family suppers.

The duke himself, meanwhile, became intrigued by certain scientific and technological developments. The air was, literally, full of new inventions. When the aeronaut Jean-Pierre Blanchard devised a helicopter-like machine that rose 80 feet above the ground, Chartres offered him 20,000 livres if he could fly it from a hilltop launch site into the duke's own gardens at Le Raincy,

north of Paris. After Blanchard failed, the duke shifted his attentions to the balloon experiments that were being undertaken by the brothers Joseph-Michel and Jacques-Étienne Montgolfier.

As the brilliantly colored orbs headed skyward, Chartres became not merely enthusiastic but obsessive. He set up a ticket booth at the Palais Royal for spectators who wished to view the ascents at close quarters, rode his horse across the countryside in the very shadow of the balloons, and sent his dinner guests into fits of ribald laughter by distributing miniature balloons, in phallic shapes, as airborne party favors.

Out at Versailles, the queen was equally intrigued by these aeronautical experiments. She persuaded her husband—who had previously contented himself with reading about the new developments in the press and the police reports—to take a more active interest. Why should Chartres, whom she loathed, have all the fun and glory? Inevitably Versailles and the Palais Royal backed different horses: The king and queen favored hot-air balloons; Chartres supported those powered by hydrogen. In the end, the duke's preferred balloon flew faster and higher.

In November 1785 Philippe the Stout died. The duc de Chartres now became duc d'Orléans, premier prince of the blood. For the new incumbent, the prestige of the dukedom may have been less important than the wealth that came with it—huge territories and a phenomenal yearly income of six to seven million livres. The free-spending duke's legion of creditors breathed sighs of relief. So did the duke himself, who celebrated his inheritance by completing the developments at the Palais Royal. All Paris rushed in to join the fun. The concession holders prospered. So did their princely landlord.

Orléans, having acquired a taste for entrepreneurship, extended his interests into the new chemical industries. And he was not the only noble of the day prepared to soil his patrician hands with commerce. His father-in-law, the duc de Penthièvre, owned metal foundries; other dukes and princes became involved in textiles and coal mining. The powdered idlers at Versailles might laugh up their satin sleeves, but their commercially minded brethren had the advantage over them. They were finding not only new sources of wealth, but new identities. They had less of a social and financial stake in the old regime, less reason to dread its disintegration. And the old regime was indeed lurching toward a precipice. By 1787 France was almost bankrupt. The extravagances of king and court had bled the country dry. Louis and his ministers were convinced that the only way to improve the situation was to raise new taxes.

From all parts of the realm came demands for a meeting of the Estates-General, a body of representatives drawn from the dominant sectors of French society—the First Estate, the clergy; the Second Estate, the nobility; and the Third Estate, comprising everyone else, including the peasantry, laborers, and the bourgeoisie. At a so-called *séance royale* of the Court of Peers on November 19, Louis presented his nobles with a proposition: He would allow the Estates-General to convene in exchange for an immediate 120 million livres of new taxation.

Orléans was having none of it. He knew—so did they all—that the Estates-General's ancient right of assembly was not subject to royal approval. He rose to his feet and declared, "Sire, this is against the law!" The words ripped through the chamber like a gunshot. Never before had a prince of the blood stood up before a king and told him that there were legal or constitutional limits to his power.

Louis was in no mood for challenges. Once again he banished this troublesome duke. When all the members of the Paris parlement supported Orléans, the king announced that they were exiled too. But within a few months he was forced to allow them home again, and a date was set for a meeting of the Estates-General in May 1789.

When the clerics and nobles of the First and Second Estates tried to limit the number of Third Estate representatives at this upcoming assembly, Orléans stood against

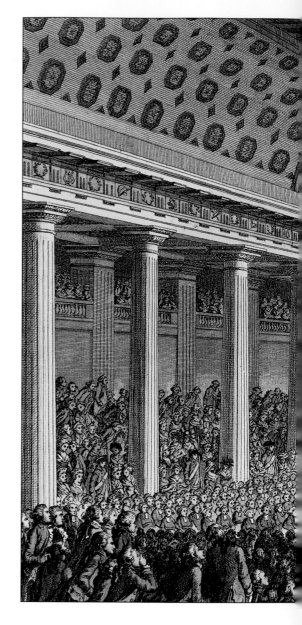

In hopes of stemming France's financial crisis while faced with opposition to his efforts at economic reform, Louis XVI convened this meeting of the Estates-General in May 1789. It was a decision that proved fatal for the monarchy.

reforms, libel his foes, and in an early version of political spin doctoring, improve his public image.

But Orléans, for all his enthusiasm, tended to favor talk over action. "To prepare the Revolution," declared his friend, the radical campaigner Jacques-Pierre Brissot, "one needed good morals, energetic pamphlets, everything that could tie the prince to a people weary of despotism. And nothing more ever happened than making plans in the middle of profligate dinners, served by lackeys who were, for the most part, spies."

Eventually, however, the duke would make those gestures that would show he was no mere aristocratic tourist in the dangerous country of revolution. To establish his republican credentials, he renounced his old aristocratic identity, Philippe, duc d'Orléans, in favor of the militant and ultramodern Philippe Égalité—Philip Equality. His residence also underwent a name change: Palais Royal, in these antimonarchist times, was clearly unthinkable. Instead, it was officially

them. He turned his back on these conservative elites, just as he had turned his back on the king. He threw in his lot with those demanding more radical change. Although not himself the most creative thinker, Orléans had the resources and the will to buy himself idea men and journalists, including the celebrated Choderlos de Laclos, author of the notorious novel *Les Liaisons dangereuses,* a chronicle of aristocratic lechery and double-dealing. The duke used Laclos and his ilk to promote his favored

rechristened the Garden of the Revolution.

The new name was apt. From this revolutionary garden had come the throng who marched on Versailles in October 1789 to arrest the king and queen. Philippe Égalité would soon exact his bittersweet recompense for all the humiliations and sentences of exile Louis XVI and his grandfather, Louis XV, had heaped upon him. When the time came to sentence the king, this antiroyalist prince of the blood would be one of those who voted for his death.

The New Middle Class

According to Diderot's *Encyclopédie,* a bourgeois was a "person who ordinarily resides in a town." Generally, however, the word referred to a person in the middle class, the group between laborers and the nobility. This group also comprised several classes of its own, from the petite bourgeoisie, including merchants who lived on modest incomes, to the haute bourgeoisie, with its financiers whose wealth equaled or exceeded that of the nobility, with whom they often intermarried.

The bourgeoisie forged a new culture in the 18th century. Like the nobility, they employed servants to do their menial work, and they outfitted themselves and their homes with fine and expensive goods. But unlike the nobles, they actively pursued financial gain and sought to create a haven in family life, with husbands and wives living together and raising their own children. Their growing numbers helped fuel a building boom in Paris between 1760 and 1790, when the area encompassed by the capital tripled in size. As one writer marveled, "Immense blocks of buildings rise from the ground as if by magic, and new districts are composed of the most magnificent mansions." Some of these new homes are shown below in a scene of city life near the Pont-Neuf, a bridge over the Seine.

Strengthening Family Bonds

A fashionable family drinks cocoa in front of the fireplace with their children, one of whom brings an assortment of toys to the table.

A governess gives her young charge a last dusting off before he leaves to visit his tutor.

The practice among aristocratic families of arranging marriages for either political or economic reasons trickled down to some degree into the middle class, but for the most part, bourgeois marriages were based on affection. The upper classes alternately scorned such marriages or romanticized them, much as the philosophe and baron Montesquieu did when he wrote, "We can boast of many marriages which turn out happily, and of many very virtuous women. The people to whom we refer live in unbroken harmony, they are liked and respected by everybody." As usual, the truth was somewhere in between: Most bourgeois couples lived together and tried to make the best of it.

At the urging of Enlightenment thinkers like Jean-Jacques Rousseau, French bourgeois families began to rediscover the joys of raising children at home. More mothers began to breast-feed their own children rather than sending them off for two years to wet nurses in the country, where the mortality rate was alarming. In addition, Rousseau, in the novel *Émile*, which espoused his educational theories, broke with tradition and condemned the practice of sending children away to boarding schools. He strongly advocated teaching young people at home—with the help of a governess or tutor—where a child's moral nature and unique personality could best be nurtured.

As visiting family members admire the new baby, an older child offers sugared almonds to the parrot.

A woman and child amuse themselves in a well-equipped kitchen
while the cook prepares a meal.

Running a Household

Back from the market, a kitchenmaid lays down her parcel of fresh bread and another servant chats with a visitor at the door.

Bourgeois families generally sent their clothes and linens out to a laundress, like the one at left, who did the washing in her home.

Middle-class families, like their aristocratic counterparts, relied on servants to do much of the household work, from cooking and cleaning and shopping and mending to waiting on the family and guests. The petit bourgeois family made do with a single female servant, but wealthier households employed many, and one indication of a family's wealth was the number of male servants who worked for them. Most servants came from the country, and their term of employment was generally less than one year. They often lived in their employers' homes, sometimes even sleeping in their bedrooms, although it was becoming more fashionable for wealthy bourgeois to house their servants out of sight, in attics, basements, and annexes.

Though the servants did the work, it was the mistress of the house who was responsible for making sure everything ran smoothly. Writing about the ideals of household management, the marquis d'Argenson declared, "In a house everything ought to seem so well regulated that the master or mistress of the house have only a sign to make for their guests to be well waited on." To accomplish that, he continued, the mistress "must devote some portion of her time, when she is alone with her servants, to giving her orders, and seeing after the expenditure. She ought to know what each object costs and what becomes of it."

In her boudoir, a fashionable lady sits at her dressing table and examines samples of ribbon brought by a young visiting saleswoman.

Alone and with her curtains drawn, a young woman falls into a reverie, undoubtedly inspired by the novel that she has just set down on her dog's elegant kennel.

A maid delivers coffee and a love letter to the mistress, who bathes, semiclad, in a canopied tub, a cloth protecting her from the touch of metal.

A Woman's Private Retreat

A boudoir, consisting of a bedchamber, dressing room, bathroom, and sometimes an attached servant's room, served as an aristocratic lady's private retreat, where she could read, sleep, and entertain close friends. Bourgeois women, wishing to emulate the upper classes, arranged their rooms similarly if they could. When there was enough space, husbands and wives occupied separate quarters, and the wife's boudoir tended to be grander than the husband's bedroom. And since women used their boudoirs as sitting rooms for guests, beds were placed in niches, with curtains enclosing them for both warmth and privacy.

Curtains were used for privacy in the bath as well, and they could also be drawn around the tub for a steam-bath effect. Bathtubs were filled with buckets of hot water or, in the latest design, by means of a boiler behind the bathroom supplying hot water through pipes in the wall. Although chamber pots were still widely used, a new invention, the water closet, imported from England, could be found in some fashionable homes, and was referred to as the "lieux à l'angloise," or "English place."

The little dogs fancied by so many aristocratic and bourgeois women had their place in the boudoir as well. Their kennels were decorated in keeping with the rest of the room and sometimes were even padded and lined with velvet.

In an elegant drawing room, a companionable group relaxes while listening to a gentleman read one of Molière's plays aloud.

Entertaining Friends

A gentleman watches women enjoy an after-dinner round of cards by candlelight while a servant lays another log on the fire and a couple converse on the sofa.

An English visitor to Paris wrote that "pleasure" was the "great business" of the capital of France, and among 18th-century well-to-do Parisians, one of the greatest pleasures was entertaining at home. At-home amusements included convivial suppers, games, conversation, and music. In his comedies, the playwright Florent Dancourt poked fun at bourgeois women's desire to play the great hostess: When one character's husband complained about her frivolous plans, she replied, "I shall only want music three times a week; on the other three evenings there will only be a little lansquenet and ombre [card games], followed by a large supper." That would leave, she continued, "one day, which will be devoted to conversation; we shall read clever books, discuss the news, and, in fact, employ ourselves the whole day upon 'things of the mind.'"

Ambitious hostesses created a demand for luxurious home furnishings. Mirrors, whose manufacturing process was a secret held until the 16th century by the Venetians, began to brighten drawing rooms with reflected candlelight coming from crystal chandeliers and etched-glass lanterns. Comfortable upholstered sofas and chairs with down-filled cushions accommodated a lady's voluminous skirts and encouraged long conversations. One woman spent so much time sitting that she declared, "Without this chair, I'd be lost."

Romancing couples linger at the table after an intimate supper in a small, private dining area away from the eyes of the servants.

CHAPTER TWO

The Shape of Things to Come

Madame Geoffrin, seated beside a dozing guest at the far right in this portrayal of her famous salon, listens as an actor reads a play by Voltaire beneath the author's bust. Among those in attendance are the philosophes Rousseau and d'Alembert, as well as Madame Geoffrin's friend and fellow salonnière, Julie de Lespinasse (at left, front).

 "That blind and vaporous old woman," Julie de Lespinasse grumbled to herself as she adjusted the angle of the painting and stepped back from the wall to eye the effect. How dare Madame du Deffand, how dare the ungrateful old dragon question her loyalty and accuse her of stealing the affection of their mutual guests. How could she suspect such a thing, after all these years, after all that Julie had done for her and her salon, Julie thought, seething, a dismissive wave of her hand adding emphasis to her words.

As she moved from room to room in her new apartment, shifting a chair here and straightening a cushion there in preparation for her own debut as a *salonnière,* Julie could not help but wonder at the turn of events that had led to her falling-out with the mercurial Madame du Deffand. After all, Julie thought, she had spent 10 years of her life with that woman, 10 years, only to be shown the door with less consideration than the lowliest servant might have expected. Ten years, during which Julie had catered to the older woman's every whim, had received the salon's guests and kept them entertained, and had, in addition, served as Madame's eyes after the old hen completely lost her sight. And was it Julie's fault that Madame's gentleman friend, the man

she called her *chat sauvage,* or wildcat, the famous mathematician Jean Le Rond d'Alembert, had displayed more than a friendly interest in the aging salonnière's pretty young protégée? Surely Julie could not be blamed for the misguided yearnings of a middle-aged man's heart.

Still, Julie would be the first to acknowledge her debt to her erstwhile companion, in no small part because that companion also happened to be her aunt. Moreover, Madame du Deffand had intervened at a serendipitous moment in her niece's life, just as the young woman—unutterably miserable at the time in her capacity as governess to a half sister's children—had been contemplating taking the veil, one of the few means of escape open to a girl of illegitimate birth. Madame had offered Julie both a position and a place to stay, and had promised to treat her young charge with "politeness, and even with compliment." In return, Julie was always to show the "utmost truth and sincerity." To do less, warned her aunt, was to discover that "I am without mercy."

All that, however, was 10 years ago, back in 1754, and if in the intervening decade Julie had unwittingly overstepped the limits of Madame du Deffand's mercy, she had also done much in that time to overcome the constraints of her own illegitimacy. In doing so, Julie had achieved the kind of independence few women, let alone women of her own misbegotten station, could ever hope to achieve. Madame's salon was the gathering place of the philosophes, those progressive thinkers who gave this *siècle des lumières*—this "century of lights"—its incandescence. It was also one of the few places where a woman of an independent mind could shine. Here, in an atmosphere of formal conviviality, where serious discourse was leavened by wit and governed by manners, a woman could command respect and might expect to be treated as the intellectual equal of the learned thinkers in her company, men who were the leading citizens

Like most women who became salonnières, Julie de Lespinasse learned the art of conversation and mediation by serving an apprenticeship, in her case at the salon of her aunt, Madame du Deffand. Lespinasse's own salon was known for its forthright discussion of the controversial issues of the day.

of the Enlightenment's borderless republics of letters and science.

But for Julie de Lespinasse, glancing around her white-paneled drawing room and its suite of comfortable furniture, this day had not come soon enough. Now, as a salonnière in her own right, with several small pensions to shore up her financial freedom, she could use the social skills she'd mastered under Madame's tutelage to conduct her own salon on her own terms. As for Madame du Deffand, thought Julie, the old woman's overly pampered dog, her doddering suitors, and the quacks she mistook for physicians could tend to her needs; Julie herself, pursing her lips to blow a wisp of dust from a bust of Voltaire atop her roll-top desk, had had enough.

With a malicious smile, Julie recalled how lucky she'd been to find an apartment hardly more than a block from her aunt's, knowing that her very proximity would infuriate the older woman. And the apartment itself—the upper two floors of a three-story town house—was quite literally a step up. Even the most unceremonious of the philosophes would consider its location more hospitable than Madame's rented quarters. For Julie's aunt, not unlike many another unwedded woman, had for some years taken her lodgings in a convent, and the address alone had been enough to scare off many of the freethinking regulars of Madame's salon.

Julie could be sure that at least one of the regulars who frequented Madame du Deffand's was now certain to grace her own salon with his company. Indeed, rumor had it that Madame had given her chat sauvage, d'Alembert, an ultimatum and that forced to choose between his allegiance to du Deffand and his love for Julie, he had chosen the latter. Others, no less admiring of the young hostess's charms than d'Alembert, were likely to make the same choice, especially given Julie's announced intention to make her home available every evening, rather than just one night a week as Madame did. Unlike her aunt, however, Julie had no plans to entertain her guests to all hours of the night; instead, she had already made it clear that they could arrive at five but should look to the door by nine, thereby sparing herself the expense of providing them with dinner.

Still, though the evening might be short on food, Julie promised herself that it would always be long on conversation. As for the topics of that conversation, Julie hoped that every evening's discussion would be open ended; religion, philosophy, politics—all would be fair game.

Openness was also behind her decision not to confine her guestlist to just males, even though many other salons consisted only of a salonnière and what Rousseau disparagingly called "a harem of men." She herself had long been a Wednesday-afternoon regular at Madame Geoffrin's salon, her attendance anticipating fellow salonnière Suzanne Necker's pointed observation that "women fill the intervals of conversation and of life, like the padding that one inserts in cases of china." Although "they are valued as nothing," Necker would further argue, "everything breaks without them."

By 1774, Julie de Lespinasse had padded many a case of china since her first summer as a salonnière 10 years before. Ten years of orchestrating evening conversations had in fact callused a spirit most of her guests had always thought irrepressible, so much so that she confided to her latest lover, the 31-year-old comte Jacques-Antoine de Guibert, that he alone made her life bearable. "In the midst of the sorry writers, smatterers, fools and pedants, among whom I spent my day," she confessed that year in a moment of pronounced despair, "I thought of you alone."

Those same 10 years had made Julie's salon the most celebrated in all of Paris, and its illustrious guestlist had secured her reputation as the "muse of the *Encyclopédie*," that multivolume compendium of all human knowledge that became the centerpiece of the Enlightenment in France. Still, she would not be swayed by the blandishments of all those "sorry writers." Her own

A group of well-to-do Parisians drink tea, socialize, and enjoy the music at this concert in the home of the prince de Conti. The harpsichordist on this occasion was the seven-year-old Mozart, who, feeling somewhat ignored at such performances, later complained, "I was forced to play to the seats and tables and walls."

face told a different story, she knew that, and to linger before a mirror was to read it with a painful clarity: her brown hair, flecked with gray, now that she had seen the last of 42; her pitted cheeks, reminders of the smallpox that had almost killed her just months after welcoming her first guests in 1764; the lined forehead, which, to her at least, betrayed an intimacy with despair; dark eyes, made darker by the memory of her attempted suicide 16 years ago; and overall, a pallor that an acute observer would recognize as evidence of dependence on opium.

But in Julie's view, the drug was not a problem; it—and the youthful comte de Guibert, of course—helped ease the passage of her days. "How strange it feels to be lifeless and yet alive!" Julie marveled in a letter in which she also admitted, with no hint of regret, that "for two hours this afternoon I was unable to identify a single face." And yet, her abuse of opium—she consumed as many as four grains several times a day—was hardly considered unusual. Many people indulged in the habit, and the grains—tiny opium pills mixed with sugar or marshmallow—could be bought over the counter at any of the capital's better perfume shops. "It brought me peace of mind," she wrote of this small consolation, a peace of mind that was to her "more precious than sleep."

At the worst of times, Julie had been known to dose herself with a few grains before the sun could brighten her windows. Happily, however, this day was not one of those, and she had moved through the morning with little more than coffee as a stimulant, with the passing hours marked by the comings and goings of one or another of her four servants tidying up after last night's gathering. The afternoon proved equally fleeting, and before she knew it, Julie, her chin cupped in one hand, her face framed in an open window, was listening expectantly for the sound of hoofbeats that would announce the arrival of the evening's first guest. Outside her town house, figures moved silently along the Rue Saint-Dominique as the sun dipped nearer the familiar Paris skyline of domed cathedrals and spired churches. This had to be her favorite time of day, Julie thought idly to herself, her eyes following the impromptu gavotte of a trio of passersby deftly sidestepping the horse droppings in the cobbled street. And this last hour before her nightly soiree was never more delicious than it was now, deep in the languor of the French summer, with the air all but liquid in the August heat and the afternoon light a golden amber.

Though she rarely knew on any evening who would arrive first, Julie was not surprised when a mud-splattered carriage slowed to a stop and out stepped a young man known, by name and reputation, as *le bon Condorcet,* a salon regular these last five years. The gifted mathematician's right foot seemed to meet the curbstone just as the drawing-room clock tolled five, but Julie lingered for a moment at the window until she heard him climb to the second floor. In a minute, maybe less, she would begin a well-practiced routine: immediate smiles, sometimes heartfelt, sometimes merely polite; pairs of kisses, one for each cheek; the patter of small talk, as one guest after another entered the room and, guided by Julie's arm, sank into a favorite chair. Indeed, Condorcet was barely ensconced in his customary *chaise* when the writer Jean-François Marmontel was escorted into the drawing room. In short order followed Anne-Robert-Jacques Turgot, the reform-minded bureaucrat, and making a rare appearance, the writer Denis Diderot, general editor of the *Encyclopédie.* Also expected, and always welcome, was the duchesse de Châtillon, and never far behind, the mathematician d'Alembert, who for almost a decade had been renting three rooms on the top floor of Julie's own apartment.

Invariably, it was the witty and brilliant d'Alembert, with his distinctively high voice, who took the lead in the evening discussions, and tonight was no exception. Julie listened intently, her face betraying no sign of the weariness she felt. A truly remarkable man, she thought to herself, and like herself, of illegitimate birth. Often she had heard him tell how, as an infant, he'd been found by the police in a wooden box on the steps of the little church of Saint-Jean le Rond; how his mother, the former nun and celebrated salonnière Claudine-Alexandrine de Tencin, adamantly refused to recognize him as her son; and how it was his cavalry-officer father, the chevalier Destouches, who had come to the child's rescue and placed the boy in the care of a Madame Rousseau, the wife of a glazier.

Left unmentioned was the fact that the newborn d'Alembert's abandonment, although deplorable, was unremarkable. Everyone in Paris knew that unwanted infants could be left on church or hospital steps. The practice was not confined to the poor, either, since some well-to-do parents, confronted with what a number of them reasoned was a squalling inconvenience, readily took the easy way out.

By all appearances, d'Alembert's unhappy start on life seemed to have had little lasting effect. An inheritance after his father's death had, in fact, ensured an education that belied his upbringing in an ordinary artisan's home. He had, moreover, been elected to the prestigious French Academy of Sciences at the age of 24, and a lifetime of accomplishment had since made him one of the most esteemed scientists of his time. But friends knew, too, that he had continued to live with his foster mother, Madame Rousseau, until he was 48, his reluctant departure prompting

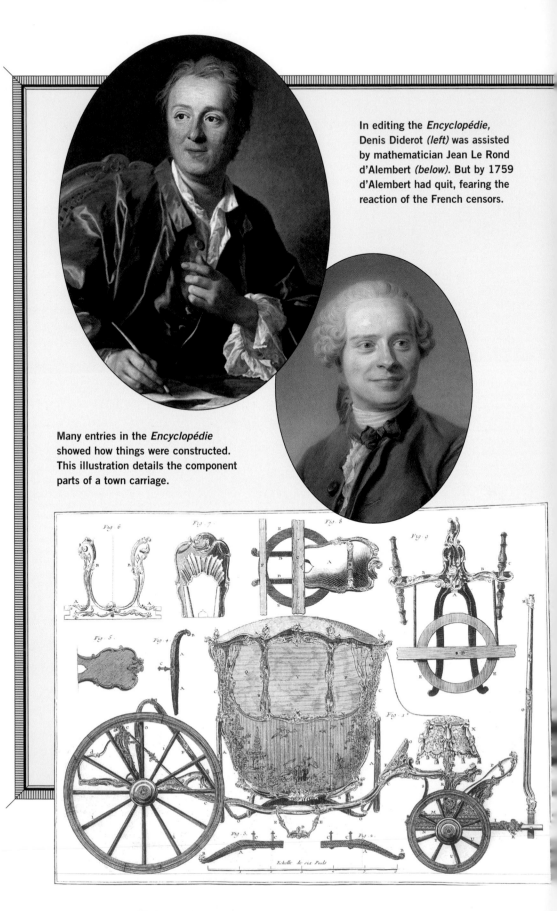

In editing the *Encyclopédie*, Denis Diderot *(left)* was assisted by mathematician Jean Le Rond d'Alembert *(below)*. But by 1759 d'Alembert had quit, fearing the reaction of the French censors.

Many entries in the *Encyclopédie* showed how things were constructed. This illustration details the component parts of a town carriage.

COMPILING THE WORLD'S KNOWLEDGE

Knowledge, according to the philosophes of the French Enlightenment, was the path to happiness. And in 1751 one of their number, the writer Denis Diderot, published the first installment of a 35-volume compendium with a simple, if perhaps unattainable, goal: to impart all knowledge. It was known as the *Encyclopédie.*

To complete his mammoth undertaking, Diderot called on the help of more than 200 of his fellow men of letters, scholars, and philosophes, each of whom contributed entries on his particular areas of expertise: d'Alembert on mathematics; Quesnay and Turgot on agriculture; Rousseau on political economy and music; Voltaire on literary criticism, history, and politics.

The *Encyclopédie* caused a sensation in Paris, stirring both political and clerical opposition, and for a time the books were suppressed. But in addition to subjects like law, government, and religion, the *Encyclopédie* also contained a wealth of useful and practical information on subjects as varied as naval tactics, surgery, ropemaking, printing techniques, tennis, and horsemanship. Eleven of the huge folio volumes were filled with informative plates that illustrated these and other topics, creating a unique record of life in 18th-century France.

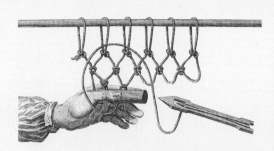

In one category of knowledge relating to occupations, Diderot illustrated different aspects of the fishing industry, including how to stitch a fisherman's net.

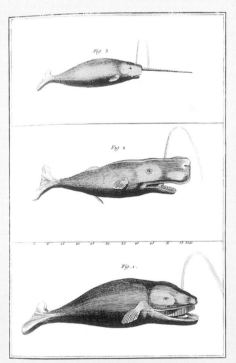

A sample from the natural sciences demonstrates water shooting from the blowholes of a narwhal and toothed and baleen whales.

This illustration demonstrates not only the art and accouterments of fencing but also the art of defending oneself—with the use of a cape—against a nighttime attack by an enemy carrying a lantern as well as a sword.

one wag to exclaim, "Oh, wondrous day! D'Alembert is weaned!"

But watching him now as he regaled her guests with impersonations of several celebrities of the day, Julie had to admit that d'Alembert was charming and, at 57, still handsome. Though he made no secret of his love for her, it was a love she could not return. Her own heart, shattered so recently by the death of her longtime lover, the Spanish nobleman Marquês José de Mora y Gonzaga, was now in the care of the comte de Guibert, whose ministrations, beginning with their liaison in the antechamber of her opera box, were having favorable effect. She might share her apartment and even her meals with d'Alembert; he could write letters for her, and he could conduct her business and financial affairs; but she did not feel for him what a mistress should.

D'Alembert's mimicry, expert as always, would have drawn

THE WORLD OF ART
Held in the Louvre *(left)*, the biennial exhibition of the Académie Royale des Peinture et de Sculpture was a thrilling event in Paris's cultural calendar. Although only academy members could enter paintings, the juried exhibitions greatly broadened public interest in art. They also gave rise to art criticism and helped spur disputes between conservative painters, who stressed draftsmanship and form, and rebels, who experimented with brushwork and color.

its usual laughter and a round of applause. Sensing an imminent lull in the conversation, Julie, exercising her prerogative as mistress of ceremonies, might then have inquired after the current plight of the philosophes, purposely inserting the phrase "republic of letters" in her question.

"The republic of letters," began d'Alembert, taking the cue and beginning to speak on a subject close to the hearts of many in the room. D'Alembert believed that the writers and thinkers who formed this phantom government must "legislate for the rest of the nation in matters of philosophy and taste," and he reminded his listeners that such public service was more necessary than ever, now that a new reign—that of Louis XVI, grandson of the old king—offered the possibility of a more enlightened government. Necessary, too, was continued vigilance against what d'Alembert's friend Voltaire dubbed *l'infâme,* the religious intolerance fueled by the Catholic Church and fanned by its supporters at court.

To d'Alembert this was all familiar territory. For decades he had argued that the

Seen here in a self-portrait, Élisabeth Vigée-Lebrun became the friend and favorite painter of Marie-Antoinette, who lobbied for her election to the academy.

republic of letters, as an intellectual community, must be autonomous and that its "citizens" must be guided by liberty, truth, and independence. This republic, d'Alembert maintained, should take as its model the community of science, just as the scientist was himself the ideal model for all intellectuals.

Such sentiments were not likely to spark dissension, not in this salon, although Julie stood ready to snuff out disagreement with the salonnière's version of diplomacy. But d'Alembert knew that his listeners supported these views, most of all his fellow mathematician Marie-Jean-Antoine-Nicolas Caritat de Condorcet.

Still in his early 30s, le bon Condorcet was, like d'Alembert, the son of a cavalry officer, though without the burden of illegitimacy. It was his particular penance, however, to have had an overzealous mother, whose suffocating sense of piety kept him in white dresses until he was eight and led her, it was said, to name the boy Marie for the Virgin Mary. This upbringing, followed by a Jesuit education, served only to mold a mind that would soon denounce all religion as superstition.

Julie could recall that when Condorcet first came to her salon, she had taken it upon herself to correct the defects of his education by steeping him in the social graces. No more nail-biting, she'd told him then, and to this day she was quick

This ceremonial apron, embroidered with Masonic emblems and symbols, was given by Lafayette to his friend and fellow Mason George Washington.

SECRET RITES OF THE MASONS

Secret societies flourished in 18th-century France and none was more popular than Freemasonry, whose 100,000 members helped disseminate Enlightenment ideas throughout the country in the years before the French Revolution.

Tracing its mythical origins back to the stoneworkers and cathedral builders of medieval Britain, and before them to the builders of the temple of Solomon, Freemasonry was a secret society complete with oaths, passwords, signs, and special handshakes. These secretive trappings, together with the symbolic use of the mason's tools—

chisel, gavel, compasses, rulers, and levels— were maintained during the 1700s when the ranks of Freemasonry were swelled by the nobles, officials, soldiers, merchants, scientists, philosophers, and clergymen who joined the philosophical and social clubs, known as lodges. The men were united in their allegiance to Freemasonry's guiding principles—toleration, reason, humanitarianism, equality, and fidelity—and by their belief in a Supreme Being: the Great Architect of the Universe.

Freemasonry rapidly spread to other parts of Europe. In Paris, the Lodge of

the Nine Sisters, which was presided over by Philippe Égalité, became the meeting ground for some of France's most prominent men. Voltaire, Montesquieu, Condorcet, d'Alembert, and the marquis de Lafayette were members, as were their visiting American brethren, ambassador Benjamin Franklin and navy captain John Paul Jones. Within the confines of the lodge they were free to discuss, in a spirit of unity and equality, the great issues of the day, making Masons, in the opinion of one French lodge member, "the only men enlightened by the true light."

At the beginning of his initiation ceremony, a blindfolded Freemasonry candidate is solemnly escorted into a Paris lodge meeting in 1740.

Swords drawn, officers of the lodge exact sacred oaths from an initiate, who lies, head covered in a shroud, on a ceremonial rug before them.

to scold him if his fingers betrayed signs of gnawing. Happily, he was less likely to chew on his lips than he had been before, and blessedly he no longer avoided making eye contact or hunched over while talking to others. As for the drifts of wig powder that were forever collecting in his ears, well, that too was less of a problem these days.

She'd had little luck, however, in convincing Condorcet that some of his many hours of study might be better devoted to the science of love. Nevertheless, Julie had herself written that le bon Condorcet was "the fairest of souls," and few men were more attuned to the inequities of the world around them or more passionate in their pursuit of social justice. He was widely known as *le volcan couverte de neige,* "the volcano covered with snow," a man whose righteous rage at any perceived threat to the public good could boil over in an instant. Indeed, Julie sometimes had to remind him to curb his tendency toward such excess. "Good Condorcet," she once admonished him, "put moderation in your tone and vigor in your substance. It is the cause of reason and humanity that you are defending."

To Condorcet, reason and humanity were the driving forces of progress, while progress was itself the hope of humanity. He would one day make his own contribution to the cause in the form of what he called "social mathematics," a science rooted in reason and the laws of probability. Condorcet hoped its practical application would help to remedy the ills of society.

Judging by the distracted look on his face, the theories of social mathematics might well have been brewing in Condorcet's mind as he listened to d'Alembert. To be sure, the older man's shrill voice—now harping on the role of *l'opinion publique* in shaping social policy—could be a distraction at times, and this was one of those times. Julie, mindful as ever of the need to keep any one person from dominating the conversation, deftly inserted herself into what was in danger of becoming a d'Alembert soliloquy and suggested that Turgot might read from his recent correspondence. So smooth was the transition that it recalled Marmontel's remark that Julie's salon was a kind of instrument that she played "with an art that bordered on genius," requiring only a word from her to produce precisely the effect she wanted.

It always amazed Julie how quickly four hours could pass. All of a sudden, it was nine o'clock, and as if on command, most of her guests were taking their leave, and those few who remained, d'Alembert among them, would soon follow.

Their early departure left Julie with time for herself, time for a visit to another salon, or time, if she wished, for her comte de Guibert. How she cherished the memory of what they referred to as the "cup of delicious poison" they sipped together, their intimacy that night at the opera. But his charms were not reserved for her; they were apparent to other women, as well. Suzanne Necker liked to tell the story of how the comte, after reading one of his own plays at her salon, touched off a mass swoon, so that, as Madame put it, "dead or dying women" had to be carried out at the end of his performance. He was not at all like the thoughtful and virtuous Mora, whose last letter, written as he lay dying of consumption, had told a heartbroken Julie, "I die for you."

No, Guibert was different. Eloquent in speech and on paper, and also, in light of his recent resumption of an affair with a former mistress, faithless. It had not even been a year since he had broken off that affair and pledged his love to Julie. Now she found herself one not of two, but of several mistresses, as the comte— how should she put it?—resumed his alley-cat ways.

And yet she would not let him go. Even after his marriage the following year in 1775, Julie would not give him up. She loved him too much, and since this was Paris, where fidelity was at best a hope and adultery at least an option, there seemed no reason to sever their relationship. At the same time, though, she hated Guibert for having made life that much less livable. "How many times must we die before dying?" she asked him in a letter.

Whatever the young comte's reply, Julie's final bout with death answered the question once and for all. By the spring of 1776, her own tuberculosis drove Julie to her bed. There, propped on a mattress four feet wide under a canopy of red damask, she would continue to receive favored visitors, albeit in a haze that owed itself as much to opium as to fever. D'Alembert, infatuated as ever, could not stay away, of course, and the good Condorcet often joined him. Julie welcomed their company now even more than she had at her evening salons.

The comte de Guibert remained a regular fixture, faithful now as he would not be before, hovering at her bedside every morning and every evening. But as April gave way to May, Julie could no longer abide his presence, not from anger or sadness, but because her constant convulsions were distorting her features and she would not have her lover remember her as anything but beautiful. Even then, however, the comte stayed as close as her bedroom door, his heart hoping that Julie would relent and allow him to come in.

It did not happen. To the end, Guibert was made to wait, although the doors opened for d'Alembert, who only left to sleep. D'Alembert's eyes spoke continuously of his grief, and as the hours lengthened toward midnight, he fought tears as a priest gave Julie the last rites. The sacrament was administered at the prodding of her late-arriving half brother, who later wrote that he had persuaded her "in spite of, in the face of, the entire *Encyclopédie*." Soon after midnight Julie murmured, "Am I still alive?" and just a little while later answered her own question with silence.

As Julie de Lespinasse breathed her last in Paris, far to the southeast, in the village of Ferney, near the Swiss border, one of the brightest lights of this century of lights, the writer and philosophe Voltaire, was himself dying—again. But as those closest to him knew, Voltaire was forever dying, even as he continued to pen scores of plays, pamphlets, dialogues, letters, and critiques, so many in the previous decade alone that Frederick the Great of Prussia had imagined that there must be more than one Voltaire.

He had moved to his Ferney estate back in 1764, the same year Julie had parted company with Madame du Deffand and established her own salon. The move had not

Bundled up to protect his frail health, the 71-year-old philosophe Voltaire works at his desk at Ferney. A prolific writer, Voltaire composed poetry, drama, fiction, satire, history, and philosophy, as well as letters by the score, both to maintain friendships during his exiles and to attack religious and political intolerance.

been wholly voluntary; some of his writings had angered the Swiss authorities, so after living for years in Geneva, he had thought it advantageous to relocate across the border to his native France. His fame aside, he was not entirely welcome there either, but Ferney's location, just three miles from the Swiss border, gave him easy access to a foreign refuge in case he heard similar rumblings from Paris.

At Ferney, Voltaire could be the lord of the manor. He governed more than a thousand acres of fields, woods, and vineyards; presided over some 30 servants; and hosted so many guests that he vented his exasperation in a letter to one confidant, "My God! Deliver me from my friends."

In fact, he had barely taken up residence at Ferney when the biographer James Boswell made his way up the treelined lane that led to the stone mansion and its extensive gardens. Voltaire, who would fend off uninvited guests with word that he was either sick or dead, ordered a servant to give the visitor the usual brush-off. But Boswell would not be deterred, and at length Voltaire made an appearance, albeit just long enough to be polite.

Feathering the air with one hand and nodding his head, the old man bade Boswell adieu and turned for his study, chuckling to himself at how quickly he had gotten rid of this latest intruder. It was the Scotsman who would have the last laugh, however. Two days later, after he petitioned Voltaire's niece for a night's lodging in the mansion's highest and coldest garret, Boswell was back at Ferney, this time as an invited guest, lodged not in a garret but in one of the château's 14 bedrooms. Proud of his new home and eager to show it off, Voltaire would have given his now-official guest a tour through the mansion itself and, despite the chill December air, the surrounding fields and winter-barren orchards of the Ferney estate. Sounding very much like an old farmer, he would have proudly told Boswell of his cows and

The marquise du Châtelet was one of the few women active in enlightened scientific circles. She translated into French Isaac Newton's *Principia Mathematica* and collaborated with Voltaire on a book about Newton's natural philosophy.

philosophes to Christianity, he soon had Voltaire at the point of fainting.

Though slight of build, the Voltaire whom Boswell came to know was an imposing figure, the fire in his eyes undimmed by his 70 years. Mornings at Ferney, he could be seen puttering around the château in a pair of cloth shoes, his knee breeches and cotton jacket topped by a flower-patterned robe. He was, as Boswell had to have noticed, scrupulously clean and very fond of cosmetics, perfumes, and pomades, though the visitor might not have guessed that his fastidious host had also renounced his razor in favor of plucking his whiskers with tweezers.

his oxen, of his wine presses, and of his sheepfold and his hundreds of beehives, all of which he personally supervised.

For his part, Boswell watched the old man with interest, charmed by Voltaire's English and his effortless wit. But try as he might, he could not reconcile the warring sides of his host's personality. For here was the great Voltaire, desperate to keep the world at arm's length, yet willing to embrace it, so long as the embrace was on his own terms. Even so, by the second day of his visit Boswell made the mistake of testing the limits of his host's graciousness. Venturing to convert this most unchurched of

Boswell's brief stay probably didn't allow time for one of Voltaire's favorite diversions, staging plays at the private theater he had built on his property. But at other times, guests and hired help alike were pressed into service as thespians of the moment, sometimes with assists from professional actors and occasionally with Voltaire himself in a leading role. And for Voltaire, each performance was yet another opportunity to thumb his nose at his nemesis, Jean-Jacques Rousseau, for whom the stage epitomized the falseness of a corrupt civilization.

But then, Voltaire knew that Rousseau was a Genevan, and what more could be expected from a place where the city's Calvinist fathers had ordered the burning of every copy of Voltaire's own *Dictionnaire philosophique*? This was the edict that prompted Voltaire's recent move across the border. But what was another move, when he had moved so often, having lived at various times in London, Paris, Potsdam, Strasbourg, and Geneva, "an old bird" with "no nest," as he liked to think of himself.

Ferney, though, might well be the nest he had sought for so long. He was happy here, he had to admit, and never more so than when he was in his garden hoeing his own cabbages or in his hothouse raising trees from seeds. It was enough to make him forget, if only temporarily, the catalog of ills—among them a nervous stomach, interminable itching, and a sluggish bladder—that plagued his days and made his nights a particular torment.

Naturally, everyone advised him to see a doctor, but a doctor, to Voltaire, was about as useful as Rousseau with a pen. True, the master of Ferney swore by a good purging, though his thrice-weekly enemas had yet to effect a permanent cure for any of

CITIZEN ROUSSEAU

Man is naturally good, and only by institutions is he made bad." So declared Jean-Jacques Rousseau in an essay published in Paris in 1755, succinctly summarizing the basic idea that ran through much of his work: that society had corrupted humanity, and only through a better society could we be improved.

Seven years later, Rousseau published *The Social Contract*, in which he speculated on just how one of society's institutions—government—should be transformed. True sovereignty, he argued, lay with the people, and the only legitimate governments were those subject to the will of the people.

The Social Contract sent shock waves through the courts of Europe. With one stroke, Rousseau denied the divine right of kings and advocated pure democracy, a form of government that almost everyone since the ancient Greeks had dismissed as dangerous and absurd. Rousseau was condemned by the Parlement of Paris, which ordered his arrest. He fled into exile, first to his native Switzerland and then to Britain. Eventually Rousseau returned to Paris and continued to write. He died suddenly in 1778, unaware of the impact his ideas on democracy would have a decade or so later when France erupted in revolution.

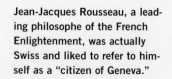

Jean-Jacques Rousseau, a leading philosophe of the French Enlightenment, was actually Swiss and liked to refer to himself as a "citizen of Geneva."

Remembered mainly as a prophet of revolution *(inset, above),* Rousseau also wrote extensively concerning the rearing and education of children. In this painting he approvingly offers wildflowers to a nursing mother.

CLUB REVOLUTIONNAIRE DES AMIS DE JEAN JAQUES

his ailments. And he drank coffee in quantities that some might consider medicinal—as many as 50 cups a day. But for Voltaire coffee was more of a pleasure, every cup harking back to those early days in Paris, when he would linger in the dimly lit Café Procope, one of hundreds of coffeehouses that served as impromptu salons. There, disguised and hidden in the shadows of a café its regulars called "the Cave," the young Voltaire would eavesdrop on neighboring tables, listening intently whenever the talk turned to his own latest play.

How long ago it all seemed now. Indeed, he had only to stroll his estate to realize just how far he had come from the Café Procope, from those days of his involuntary stays in the Bastille, from the smallpox that had nearly killed him in his 20s. "What a miserable game of chance human life is," he'd once written. He himself had managed to come away a winner, though, at least financially, his success as a writer and a string of savvy investments having years ago made him a millionaire.

Voltaire realized how lucky he was. That much-vaunted republic of letters included any number of writers whose output—much of it the *chroniques scandaleuses* that aired the sordid

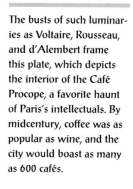

The busts of such luminaries as Voltaire, Rousseau, and d'Alembert frame this plate, which depicts the interior of the Café Procope, a favorite haunt of Paris's intellectuals. By midcentury, coffee was as popular as wine, and the city would boast as many as 600 cafés.

details of love affairs or crimes—produced very little that could be called an income. Voltaire had no use for such scribblers— "the unhappy class who write in order to live," he called them—or for their writing. "The misfortune of these men is that their fathers did not make them learn a trade," he sniffed.

Still, he did do his best to share his wealth, if not with his fellow writers, then at least with those who had learned trades. Already Voltaire had plans to develop cottage industries on his estate, and in the course of the next decade he did just that. Soon the watchmaking, jewelry, and weaving shops located there were providing jobs for hundreds of locals. And since those workers needed shelter, Voltaire also saw to it that they had homes; he even provided loans to help them buy their homes, as well as needed livestock and farming supplies. At the same time, he made his own home available to the younger residents of what he called his "odd little kingdom," inviting them in every Sunday for dancing and refreshments and taking at least as much pleasure in the merriment as the dancers themselves.

Je deviens patriarche" (I am becoming a patriarch), Voltaire wrote of his burgeoning commune at Ferney. For evidence, he could walk the streets of his personal village, savoring at every step the hum of activity in the busy workshops. As for the output of those shops, it was being snapped up by some of the most illustrious customers on the Continent and beyond; Voltaire had made sure of that by taking advantage of his many friendships with the high and the titled. Ferney clocks, watches, jewelry, and silk stockings were as likely to be found in the St. Petersburg palace of Catherine the Great as in Paris, and in the casbahs of Morocco as in the more elegant townhomes of patrician Boston.

Modestly pleased with these developments, Voltaire might have shrugged and said, "Tout va bien," or as his young Scottish friend Boswell would have put it, "All well

The police regularly banned and often destroyed books that were deemed subversive in their religion or politics, such as the volumes of the Jesuits being burned at left. Voltaire's writings often got him into trouble: His *Lettres philosophiques* were burned; his epic, *La Henriade* (shown below), was banned; and his poems lampooning the regent got him arrested.

and good." But in a country where Protestants had so often suffered at the hands of their Catholic neighbors, the man who regularly raised his pen against l'infâme could be especially proud that the residents of Ferney practiced the very toleration that he had long preached. As any visitor could see, Ferney was truly common ground and, to Voltaire, proof that all of France might one day be the same.

Of course, before that could happen, l'infâme would first have to be *écrasé*—crushed—and no one knew better than Voltaire how difficult a task that was going to be. Just look at what had happened after the publication of his *Dictionnaire philosophique*—burned in Geneva, burned in Paris, burned in Abbeville along with a poor youth convicted of blasphemy. All this because Voltaire had dared express skepticism about the Bible, because he had questioned the authority of the Catholic Church, and because he considered mere superstition much of what passed for religion? To that he could only say what he'd been saying since 1759: "Écrasez l'infâme!"

Much to Voltaire's dismay, however, the thing he called l'infâme—a religion that had superstition as its carrot and persecution as its stick—still had the upper hand. He remembered well the day that he had first heard of the unfortunate Jean Calas. Even now, cradling a cup of coffee and looking up from his desk to the peaceful scene framed in the window of his study, he could be driven to rage by the thought of that old man's cruel torture and senseless execution.

Voltaire recalled how it had been Monsieur Calas's misfortune to have been a Huguenot in a Catholic country that cared very little for those Calvinist Protestants. By law Protestants had few civil rights, limited opportunities to enter the professions, and no chance to hold public office. Moreover, death was still the fate of any clergyman caught conducting Protestant services. If such verdicts were rarely handed down in more tolerant Paris, that was not the case in the southwestern city of Toulouse, where as recently as 1761 a Huguenot pastor had been condemned to death and where Jean Calas had made his living as a linen merchant.

As everyone familiar with the case knew, Calas might still be a linen merchant, had he not attempted to pass off a grown son's suicide as a natural death. Any father might have done exactly the same, Voltaire would have argued, since taking one's life was illegal and the law required that the corpse of a suicide be hauled naked through the streets and then publicly hanged. The authorities, however, were not fooled and had promptly arrested the entire Calas family. They were arrested not for covering up a suicide, but for murder, allegedly committed to prevent the son from converting to Catholicism.

As Voltaire heard the story, what happened next was sadly predictable: a lengthy mockery of a trial, the testimony more hearsay than fact, ending with the expected guilty verdicts; an appeal that freed all but Jean Calas; and an attempt to force his confession by means of the dreaded *question ordinaire,* during which Calas's arms and legs were first stretched and then pulled from their sockets. When that failed, Calas's inquisitors began the *question extraordinaire,* the forced feeding of some four gallons of water that ballooned the accused's body to twice its normal size. Finally, Calas was cruelly broken on the wheel and, after hours of agony, throttled. Even then, however, justice had yet to be served in the eyes of the executioners, who finally roped the corpse to a stake and torched it.

To Voltaire the whole sorry episode was evidence of contemporary Christianity's basic hypocrisy, pretending to sow love while in reality reaping hate. After verifying the facts of the case and concluding that Jean Calas had been innocent, he personally set out to clear the dead man's name and summoned his friends to do the same. His call to arms to Jean Le Rond d'Alembert in September 1762 was typical: "Shout everywhere, I beg you, for the Calas and against fanaticism, for it is l'infâme that has caused their misery."

Now, almost three years after Calas's execution, Voltaire, sitting in his Ferney study, had the sense that events were finally moving toward a favorable resolution. Yet even he was not optimistic enough to believe that a decision was just months away and that the royal council would exonerate Jean Calas of guilt and order the Calas family compensated for his wrongful death. But in March 1765, when that news arrived, Voltaire wept for joy.

For as long as he lived, the man who became known as *l'homme aux Calas,* "the man of Calas," would think of the Calas case as his best work. Regrettably, however, it was not the only case of its kind, and Voltaire would soon take up the plight of the Sirvens,

Falsely accused of killing his son, the Protestant Jean Calas bids farewell to his family before his torture and execution. Outraged by what he saw as a case of religious persecution, Voltaire launched a campaign to clear Calas's name and reform the criminal-law code.

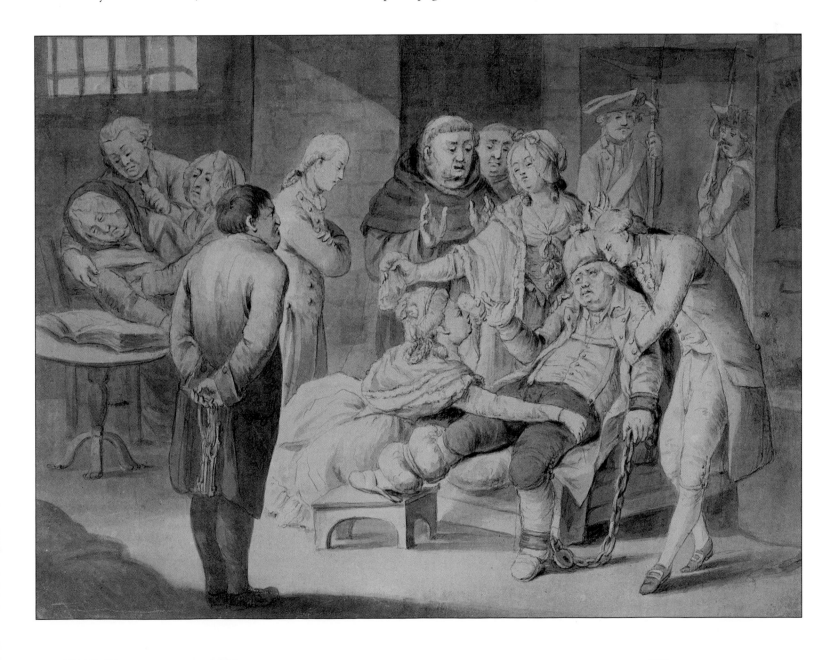

a Protestant couple sentenced *in absentia* to be hanged for supposedly murdering their daughter rather than allow her conversion to Catholicism. And just as soon as that case was resolved, and the couple acquitted, Voltaire was asked to intervene on behalf of the 19-year-old Jean La Barre, charged with blaspheming a crucifix and subsequently beheaded and burned for the "crime." For Voltaire, this latter case was especially galling, since the youth's corpse was incinerated with a copy of Voltaire's *Dictionnaire philosophique.* Worse still, a French bishop, sensing an opportunity to rid the church of one of its most influential critics, urged the court to give the book's author the same treatment. "To escape being burned," Voltaire, tongue firmly in cheek, later wrote to d'Alembert, "I am laying in a supply of holy water." His joking aside, he took the threat seriously enough to head for more earthly waters, slipping across the Swiss border to a spa at Rolle.

Voltaire died in such disfavor that his body was taken away for burial at an abbey outside Paris. During the revolution, Voltaire's coffin was returned to the capital, borne on the grand chariot at right in triumphal procession to the Panthéon, his final resting place.

In mobilizing support for these and similar cases, Voltaire was proving the power of public opinion, a relatively new force in French society. This "spirit of society," as the government minister Jacques Necker described it, which was destined to boil over at century's end in the French Revolution, had in recent decades percolated in the salons and coffeehouses, in the ethereal Académie Française, and in the reams of books, pamphlets, and newspapers that were attracting ever-larger audiences. This was welcome news to Voltaire, and all the more so since l'opinion publique was increasingly a counterforce to the French monarchy and to the church. He would later declare, "Plus les hommes sont éclairés, plus ils seront libres"—The more enlightened men are, the more free they will be. And the sworn enemy of l'infâme, l'homme aux Calas, had no doubt about the source of this new force. "Opinion governs the world," Voltaire exulted after vindicating the ghost of Jean Calas, "and in the end the philosophes govern men's opinions."

Voltaire observed that in shaping public opinion he and his fellow philosophes were also effecting a revolution. "My dear philosopher," he would inquire of d'Alembert, "doesn't this appear to you to be the century of revolutions?" But the revolution Voltaire had in mind was no mere revolution of state and certainly not the collapse of order that would be the Reign of Terror. It was a revolution in the human mind, a revolution by which

into his 70s, he took heart, nonetheless; the young people "are fortunate," he announced, "they will see great things." He hoped that among those great things would be an end to the intolerance that had resulted in the death of Jean Calas and others like him.

But the ever-dying Voltaire was still alive a decade later. By 1778 he was making plans to visit Paris, a city he had last seen 25 years earlier. But at 84 and mindful of the imminence of his death, he worried that the trip might turn out to be a "brisk jaunt to eternity." His worry seemed well founded, since he had decided to make the journey in February, and he would have to travel across the French Alps and then over the usual washboard of roads to the capital. Even in the lavender of a French summer, such a journey would be enough to give a young man pause, let alone a man who was forever telling his friends, "I am dying, literally."

No one around him wanted to believe

"To escape being burned, I am laying in a supply of holy water."

rational, practical thinking about the problems of this world would replace fanatical conflict and useless speculation about the possibilities of the next world. It was, on a grander scale, the kind of revolution he could see every day at Ferney, where his own enlightened thinking was benefiting all levels of the small society he had created. To do as much for France, for Europe, for the civilized world was, in his view, the hope of the Enlightenment. "Everything tells us that we are on the brink of one of the great revolutions of the human species," his contemporary Condorcet wrote, and Voltaire believed that the young man was right.

As the 1760s drew to a close, however, Voltaire worried that he would not live to see this revolution to its conclusion. Well

that the great man really was at the end of his life. He was, perhaps, thinner than before, and he complained that he was little more than "old parchment plastered over unanchored bones." He still had the same sparkle in his eyes, though, the same captivating smile, and the same ability to entertain his guests into the small hours of the morning.

But there could be only one opportunity to attend the premiere of his latest play, and at his age just one more chance to see Paris. And so, dying or not, he made the rounds of Ferney, bidding this one and that adieu—adieu, he promised, only for the moment. Many of the tenant farmers and resident artisans he greeted weren't convinced, and not a few of those who had come

to love the old master turned their heads to wipe away a tear.

The weeks ahead brought news back to Ferney—news of the journey, of the usual broken axles and other mishaps of the road, of crowds in the towns along the way and of larger ones in Paris itself, all clamoring for a glimpse of the renowned author of *Candide,* of the avowed foe of l'infâme—of l'homme aux Calas.

Voltaire, characteristically, took the adulation in stride. "Alas!" he said, smiling, of the cheering crowds around him, "there would be just as many to see me on the scaffold." But then he suddenly fell ill. And by month's end the man who had written entire libraries was penning the few simple words by which he wanted most to be remembered: "I die worshiping God, loving my friends, not hating my enemies, and detesting superstition."

Changes great and small had come to Paris in the quarter century between Voltaire's last two visits; he had witnessed many of them in the weeks before his death. One of the greatest of these changes was that the future City of Light had become a city of lights. In the course of his nightly peregrinations—from his lodgings at the town house of the Marquis de Villette to the theater, to the homes of old friends, to the Académie Française—Voltaire could not fail to notice the street lamps arcing overhead, their glow dispelling the gloom that in former years had turned the shadows of Paris into the haunts of petty thieves.

So vexing was the capital's crime problem that back in 1764, the very year in which Voltaire was taking up residence at Ferney and Julie de Lespinasse was setting up her own salon, the Paris police department had prevailed upon the Academy of Sciences to sponsor a competition to devise "the best means of lighting city streets, by combining brightness, simplicity of maintenance, and economy." Unfortunately, even the incentive of a cash

prize failed to attract any entries by the deadline. Undaunted, the academy doubled the prize and extended the deadline, allowing a 21-year-old chemist, Antoine-Laurent Lavoisier, time to complete his experiments and submit one of the three prizewinning reports, a 70-page paper cited by the judges for being "full of curious research and the best physics."

If any of the judges had knocked on the door of Lavoisier's Paris study in the course of this "curious research," he would have realized just how curious the young chemist's experiments were. The room's walls and windows were draped entirely in black cloth, making the study itself a kind of cave, and lurking in its interior, his brown eyes almost owl-like after some six weeks in the dark, was the scientist. He would have been immaculately groomed and clad, as was his custom, in attire more suited to the salon. Around him on tables and shelves were the paraphernalia he needed to conduct his experiments: candles of various sizes and materials, containers of different kinds of oil, and lanterns of many types, some with built-in reflectors.

Lavoisier's unstinting dedication to his work would not have surprised those who knew him. After all, this was the same Lavoisier who, beginning at age 20, kept a written record of the weather, morning and evening, for the rest of his life; who, two years earlier, had lived for a time on nothing but milk in order to study the effects of diet on health, an experiment so unhealthy that it prompted one concerned friend to caution the budding scientist to "be sparing in your studies and accept that another year on earth is better than a hundred in the memory of man"; and who would later attempt to distill earth from water, an endeavor that required him to stand watch for 101 days in order to keep the liquid's temperature just below the boiling point. The experiment proved only that prolonged boiling will dissolve glass.

Yet Lavoisier made no excuses for his myopic attention to detail and for his willingness to go to extraordinary lengths to satisfy his curiosity. His youth notwithstanding, he understood that

Antoine Lavoisier, originator of the Chemical Revolution, and his wife, Marie Anne, posed for this portrait by Jacques-Louis David. Having also served as a tax collector, Lavoisier would be arrested and executed at the height of the Reign of Terror.

science in this second half of the 18th century was more arena than field of pursuit and that to succeed as a scientist was to compete among scientists. He also believed that scientists, like writers, formed their own cultural community, a republic of science as it were. And though he yearned to make the discoveries that would bring him personal recognition, science for Lavoisier had the nobler goal of improving the common good, as he had pointed out in his streetlight report.

The reserved and bookish Lavoisier, destined to be among the founders of modern chemistry, had been trained as a lawyer, not as a scientist, and was the son of a distinguished advocate. Antoine's father expected his son to follow him into the family profession, and the young man dutifully fulfilled that expectation. But even in law school, Antoine made time to attend lectures in chemistry and physics, and the more time he devoted to it, the more he realized that he had found his calling.

Yet Lavoisier knew that it was not enough merely to answer the call. A scientist in France must also be a member of the Academy of Sciences, which, in addition to conferring prestige, carried the prospect of a stipend. Membership, however, was by election to a vacancy, preferably on the basis of a record of achievement. And while his own accomplishments were limited to a gold medal in a streetlight competition and a paper describing his analysis of gypsum, that did not deter him from campaigning for membership in 1766. Lavoisier lost, but he would not lose a second time.

By 1775, recently married and more recently appointed *régisseur des poudres,* a commissioner of gunpowder, Antoine Lavoisier was, by his own admission, less his father's son and more his own man. The past decade had in fact brought him several more benchmarks of personal and professional accomplishment: a home of his own; a growing body of scientific papers; a lucrative share in the General Farm, a company composed of a group of financiers who speculated on the profits they would make by buying the right to collect indirect taxes for the government; and, in 1768, when he was not yet 25, election to the Academy of Sciences.

In Lavoisier's own mind, his election to the academy had always been a foregone conclusion; his marriage, on the other hand, had come as something of a surprise. He would never have dreamed back in 1771 that he would find himself the groom in an arranged marriage or that his intended would be the daughter of one of his partners in the General Farm. Even so, Lavoisier was pleased that his bride, Marie Anne Paulze, though not yet 14 at the time, was attractive and mature for someone so young. He was even more delighted that she took an immediate interest in his work, becoming first his pupil and later his partner.

As for his new position as commissioner of gunpowder, this, too, had been somewhat unexpected, although entirely in keeping with his belief that the best science was that which could be applied to practical needs. The job called for a combination of skills. As an administrator, he would manage France's production of gunpowder, a commodity always necessary and often in short supply, owing partly to frequent wars and partly to a shortage of a key ingredient, potassium nitrate, also known as niter, a derivative of the naturally occurring saltpeter. As a scientist, he was charged with finding some means of furnishing the gunpowder mills with a continuous supply of saltpeter.

Traditionally, saltpeter had been "farmed" by scraping it from the places where it naturally collected: on the damp floors and walls of barns, privies, and stables, wherever limestone surfaces were exposed to the vapors emanating from excrement and rotting vegetation. Prior to the establishment of the Royal Gunpowder Administration, the collection of saltpeter and the production of gunpowder had been assigned to a group of private investors operating under royal license. This group was authorized to commandeer saltpeter wherever it could be found, disregarding, as circumstances dictated, the rights of the property

Well-heeled visitors inspect work at a tobacco factory. The production, importation, and sale of tobacco was a lucrative enterprise controlled by the General Farm, the tax-collection company in which Lavoisier was a partner. A popular stimulant, tobacco was ground and inhaled as snuff, twisted into plugs for chewing, or shredded and smoked in pipes.

This giant lens, designed by a committee of scientists that included Lavoisier, concentrated solar heat for experiments on combustion. Its operator wears dark glasses to protect his eyes. A few years earlier, Lavoisier had used a similar device to burn diamonds, an experiment that would lead to his discovery of oxygen.

owner—a system that was rife with corruption. Lavoisier's Royal Gunpowder Administration was intended to put an end to the abuse of power inherent in this system and, if possible, to develop a technique for the artificial cultivation of saltpeter.

Lavoisier's success on both counts could be measured just a year later in a gunpowder surplus that would allow France to supply the American colonies in their war with Great Britain. In the meantime, the obligations of his job did not stop him from helping Marie furnish their new home—one of the perquisites of his new position—on the grounds of the Paris Arsenal. By the spring of 1776 they were ready to move in.

The young couple could not have asked for better accommodations—a private apartment in a four-story mansion, a large library, and upstairs in the cavernous, high-ceilinged attic, a fully equipped laboratory that would become one of the most celebrated in Europe. Excitedly, Lavoisier mapped out his new schedule. He intended to spend his mornings in the laboratory, from six o'clock until eight. The rest of the day he would devote to his responsibilities as gunpowder commissioner, to his investment in tax collecting, and to the demands of the Academy of Sciences. By seven o'clock each evening, however, he would be a scientist again, climbing the stairs to the attic with a spring in his step that belied the full day of work behind him and spending another three hours in a veritable china shop stocked with thousands of beakers and flasks and hundreds of instruments.

Although most of his days began and ended with precious laboratory time, Lavoisier soon came to live for Saturdays, "a blissful day," as Marie would remember. All day, stopping only for meals, the scientist and a select group of students lost themselves in one experiment after another, the whole laboratory aboil with activity. Often, Marie joined them, her chair almost lost in the taffeta of her skirts and her head bobbing as she scratched down procedures and results, sometimes accompanying her notes with drawings of equipment and sketches of the scientists at work.

It was here, amid the constant rattle of glassware and the enthusiastic cries of his young assistants, that Lavoisier gradually refined his technique, even as he expanded his interests. For him, every experiment was as much an exercise in precision as it was a search for truth. Indeed, his emphasis on accuracy in weighing and measuring was, on its own, furthering the development of chemistry, so that it was no longer just a qualitative science, but a

could this phlogiston have negative weight? Most perplexing of all, why had so many reputable scientists bought into a theory that itself appeared to have negative weight?

Lavoisier did not yet have the answers, but he was already alert to their significance. "The importance of this object," he had written in 1773, when he first outlined what would ultimately be a 20-year-long research project, "seems likely to cause a revolution in physics and chemistry."

Marie Anne Lavoisier had never doubted that her husband was onto something. The trouble was, he was not alone. Carl Wilhelm Scheele in Sweden, Joseph Priestley in England, Pierre Bayen right here in France, and others were all eager to be the first to prove

"You know that those who start the hare do not always catch it."

quantitative science. Moreover, it was in hands like his that chemistry was finally shaking off the influence of Aristotle's theory of four elements—the time-honored fire, water, earth, and air—and taking its place in a world that was still learning to accept the theories of Isaac Newton.

For years now, in fact, Lavoisier had been focusing his investigations on the nature of combustion and the composition of air. Why was it, he kept asking himself, that when something burned, the products of combustion weighed more than the original material had? How could that be, he wondered, when combustion, by its very nature, destroyed matter? And if, as the German physicist George Stahl maintained, all matter contained phlogiston, that invisible substance said to be freed in the course of combustion, why didn't the products weigh less than the reactants? How

or disprove the existence of phlogiston and, with that breakthrough, to win a place in the history of science. For that reason, Marie had wept with relief a year ago, in 1775, when her husband disproved the existence of phlogiston and, as she later recalled, "created the theory that immortalized its author."

Lavoisier's theory was actually a synthesis of many competing theories and near enough to Priestley's own recent discovery of "dephlogisticated air" that the Frenchman's English counterpart could be heard crying foul all the way across the Channel. Lavoisier dismissed Priestley's claims with a laugh, telling a mutual acquaintance, "My friend, you know that those who start the hare do not always catch it."

In his report to the academy in April 1775, Lavoisier called his own discovery "pure air." By the following year, working in his new laboratory at the Arsenal, he had determined that air was not a pure substance, but a compound, one-sixth of which was "eminently breathable," with the rest *mofette,* or "unfit." But questions remained, questions that Lavoisier systematically answered over the remainder of the decade. He ultimately deduced that combustion was a chemical reaction; that "eminently breathable air" was a reactant in combustion, its weight accounting for the increased weight of the product; that the product was an acid; and that "eminently breathable air" was actually what he named *oxygine,* an "acid generator." Warming to the task, he daringly proposed that the act of breathing was itself a kind of combustion, one that required the so-called oxygine and that generated heat.

The pace of Lavoisier's many activities had become so feverish, it seemed that he himself might combust. But he was still in his 30s, with a

German-born physician Franz Anton Mesmer believed that healing could occur by tapping into the powers of animal magnetism present in all human bodies. Mesmer seemed particularly interested in female bodies and often treated the wealthy women of Europe in closed-door sessions.

A group of fashionable Parisians gathers round a lidded tub filled with Mesmer's magnetized water. At right, one participant swoons after being treated.

THE ANIMAL MAGNETISM OF FRANZ MESMER

According to physician Franz Mesmer, all matter in the universe was suspended in a magnetic fluid over which the planets exercised a strong gravitational pull. Illness was the consequence of an imbalance of this fluid in the body. The remedy, Mesmer maintained, was to pass magnets over patients, who then went into a trance, often accompanied by convulsions, and were pronounced cured.

To treat the large numbers who flocked to his Paris salon, Mesmer constructed several lidded tubs called *baquets,* around which as many as 30 people could be magnetized at once. The tubs held bottles of magnetized water in a slush of damp sand, iron filings, and crushed glass. Hands gripped hands to form a chain, and knees were pressed to knees while the effects of the charged fluid supposedly passed from the baquet to the patients huddled around it.

The scientific establishment was highly skeptical of Mesmer's claims. In 1784 a royal commission, which included such eminent scientists as Antoine Lavoisier and American ambassador Benjamin Franklin, examined mesmerism. It concluded that Mesmer's technique was illusory and its effects nonexistent. Any healing, said the commission, owed itself to the power of suggestion, not to "animal magnetism." Disgraced, Mesmer departed for Switzerland, where he died in poverty in 1815.

In this contemporary cartoon, Mesmer's supporters flee as Academy of Sciences member Benjamin Franklin *(above, left)* brandishes a report condemning mesmerism.

young man's stamina, and he somehow found the time and the energy to conduct his experiments even as he continued his other pursuits. One of those pursuits continued to be his work on behalf of the Royal Gunpowder Administration, which now included teaching courses to workers, attracting investors, and overseeing the construction of some two dozen new gunpowder factories, saltpeter refineries, and warehouses.

If Lavoisier gave any indication that he was in need of rest, it might have been his 1778 purchase of a country retreat, Fréchines, in the Loire Valley. Yet where others might have imagined themselves peacefully adrift on the sea of wheat that made an island of his old château, Lavoisier glimpsed opportunity; where others saw cows grazing in a landscape worthy of the Louvre, he envisioned an immense outdoor laboratory and spied the chance to conduct a vast agricultural experiment. As he was to learn, science could easily enlarge the yield of French farms and improve the lot of French farmers; however, it could do little about the tax structure and market restrictions that discouraged investment in agriculture.

Antoine Lavoisier studies respiration by having an assistant breathe into a mask that funnels his "recycled air" into flasks for analysis. Marie Anne Lavoisier, seated at far right, takes notes during the experiment. After years of such investigations, Lavoisier deduced that respiration was a form of combustion, converting oxygen to carbon dioxide.

Lavoisier quickly realized that part of the problem was that wealthy farmers could make more money by lending to the government at high interest rates than they could by investing in agriculture. He knew this because, even as he sowed his own test crops at Fréchines, he was reaping the benefits of another kind of farming, the Ferme Générale, or General Farm.

Lavoisier had not hesitated when he was offered a stake in the company back in 1768. It was, after all, the kind of low-risk, high-return investment that would entice any enterprising man, especially since it was possible to triple that investment in 20 years. The idea itself was simple: Rather than collect various taxes directly, the government leased its collection services out to the General Farm, which, in turn, could collect whatever it could by any means it could; after giving the government its due according to the terms of the lease, the tax "farmers" would split the surplus as profit.

The system was unfair and hated by those it most encumbered, but it was the way things had long been done in France. Any claim it may have made on Lavoisier's conscience did not prevent him from increasing his share in the General Farm in 1771 and a second time eight years later. To his credit, however, he did on occasion look the other way rather than discipline a tax scofflaw, and some years later, in 1786, he saw to it that the *pied fourchu,* or cloven-hoof tax, a particularly odious duty levied only on Jews, was abolished. But to his eventual misfortune, his less-magnanimous activities on behalf of the General Farm would not be forgotten. Because of those activities, the revolutionaries of a future decade would sharpen the blade of the guillotine and spare Lavoisier what he called, with a touch of macabre humor, "the inconvenience of old age."

For the time being, though, science continued to serve Lavoisier well, even in his role as a tax farmer. He was proud, for example, that his knowledge of chemistry had allowed him to devise a test that could detect tobacco that had been cut with ashes by unscrupulous retailers. And he experienced a curious sense of satisfaction when, in his official capacity as tobacco inspector, he could demonstrate the test's effectiveness, striding

> ## "A husband who would wish to have sole possession of his wife would be regarded as a disturber of public happiness."

purposefully into a tobacconist's shop, wetting each sample of tobacco with fluid from a palmed vial, then watching for the telltale effervescence.

Of course, since tobacco was a taxable commodity that fell under the purview of the General Farm, Lavoisier's motivation was not entirely selfless, for the tainted tobacco, as the tax farmer in him put it, was "as injurious to the public as it is to management." More often than not, however, his notion of science employed for the public good did guide his actions. When a study revealed that runoff from cesspools was polluting the Paris drinking supply, when the quality of air in public places was called into question, when the spread of contagious diseases raised public-health concerns, Lavoisier, often at the behest of the

Academy of Sciences, was only too happy to lend his expertise.

In this regard, Lavoisier readily concurred with Condorcet that science was the engine of social progress. If society was to be transformed by a revolution of the mind, as the philosophes hoped, if life itself was truly to be bettered by Lavoisier's "revolution in physics and chemistry," then it was science that would have to take the lead.

It was an issue that was often a topic at the Lavoisiers' salon in their Arsenal apartment. There, in the opulently appointed reception rooms on the ground floor, Europe's most distinguished scientists—their numbers bolstered at times by such occasional attendees as Benjamin Franklin—gathered twice a week to exchange ideas, to weigh theory against experiment, and to read from their latest papers. Presiding over all these animated discussions was the pleasing figure of Marie Lavoisier, sometimes carrying the conversation, her presence both necessary and deserved. As much as any of the men around her, Madame Lavoisier was an accomplished scientist in her own right, "a very clever and painstaking chemist," in the words of one admiring visitor.

The appeal of Lavoisier's comely "philosophical wife," as one observer described her, made it easy to admire her, and even, as the economist Pierre-Samuel Du Pont de Nemours quickly discovered, to fall in love with her. Witty and irrepressibly cheerful himself, he had been attracted to Marie from his first visit in 1776, although she, to his frustration, proved somewhat more resistant to his charms. But time, as well as opportunity, was on his side, since Madame Lavoisier's husband was so frequently absent from home on business. By 1781 Du Pont and the chemist's wife had become lovers.

The relationship proved enduring, but Marie gave no thought to ending her marriage. There was, in fact, no need to, not in her class anyway, since an affair was a socially acceptable substitute for divorce. Besides, she and her work-distracted husband remained friends and devoted partners. For his part, as a man

of the Enlightenment, Lavoisier would have been familiar with Montesquieu's dictum that "a husband who would wish to have sole possession of his wife would be regarded as a disturber of public happiness, and as a fool who should wish to enjoy the light of the sun to the exclusion of other men."

The winds of revolution were already swirling in the streets of Paris when Lavoisier published his *Elementary Treatise on Chemistry*, a compendium of all that was known of his "new chemistry." He had devoted a large part of 1788 to its writing but was somewhat put off early the following year when the publisher delivered the first copies. Strangely, the book consisted of a single thick volume, rather than the set of two thinner volumes he had been expecting.

If the binding was a disappointment, the content was a source of sheer pride. A full year later, as he was packing up a pair of copies for shipment to Benjamin Franklin, Lavoisier couldn't help but heft one of the heavy books in his hands. He leafed again through the pages, pausing at this chapter and that, the writer's pleasure mingling with a reader's curiosity. He lingered again over the plates, each engraving so splendidly executed by Marie. Then, smiling, the scientist closed the book, the two halves meeting with a satisfying thud, and reached for a sheet of writing paper and a quill.

"As you will see in the preface," he scrawled to Franklin, "I sought to reach the truth by linking facts, to eliminate argument as much as possible . . . and replace it by the torch of observation and experiment." Lavoisier hesitated, then finished his thought: "Here then is the revolution that has taken place in an important branch of human knowledge." He looked up again, his eyes drawn to a nearby window, his thoughts turning to that other, ever more violent revolution. "An accomplished fact," as he now confided to Franklin, "and, hence, irreversible." There was indeed no turning back, and soon, no chance to save himself.

A Scientific Revolution

During the Age of Reason, an understanding of the sciences was considered an integral part of the knowledge acquired by every educated Frenchman and -woman. As evidence of her interest, Madame de Pompadour instructed her portraitist to paint her with a telescope and mathematical instruments scattered at her feet. Fashionable Parisians kept scientific books on their bed tables. Occasionally, they installed in their homes handsomely crafted scientific instruments, such as the celestial globe known as an armillary sphere *(right)*. In a stage performance, one character refused to elope with her lover, exclaiming, "What! And leave behind my microscope?"

The French kings saw that there was much to gain from their nation's interest in science. Beginning with Louis XIV and his minister Jean-Baptiste Colbert, the monarchy established a network of national institutions to support and expand the scientific revolution. The French Academy of Sciences, the Royal Observatory of Paris, and the Royal Gardens offered stipends to scientists, created laboratories, published and circulated their work, and sponsored their debates.

But even without the government's support, scientists worked feverishly to answer old questions and pose new ones. Others' successes added fuel to the fire of discovery, bringing about, as mathematician Jean d'Alembert wrote, "a lively fermentation of minds, spreading through nature in all directions like a river which has burst its dams." By the end of the 1700s, French physicists, mathematicians, astronomers, and natural scientists led the world in exploring the frontiers of scientific advances.

Electricity, the New Science

Although Thales of Miletus had written about static, or frictional, electricity as far back as the seventh century BC, knowledge of electricity was still rudimentary at the dawn of the 18th century. But as the curious physicists of the French Enlightenment turned their attention to this new branch of science, dramatic strides were made.

An officer in the French infantry was among the first to make a breakthrough in electrical experimentation. In his reports to the Academy of Sciences and the Royal Society of London, Charles-François Du Fay described his attempts to electrify different types of materials. He concluded that there were two kinds of electricity, which he termed vitreous and resinous. "A body of the vitreous electricity," he explained, "repels all such as are of the same electricity, and, on the contrary, attracts all those of the resinous electricity."

Du Fay's theory was presented to the public by his collaborator, experimental physicist Abbé Jean-Antoine Nollet, a prominent scientific lecturer. As part of his discourses, Nollet included demonstrations on electric-

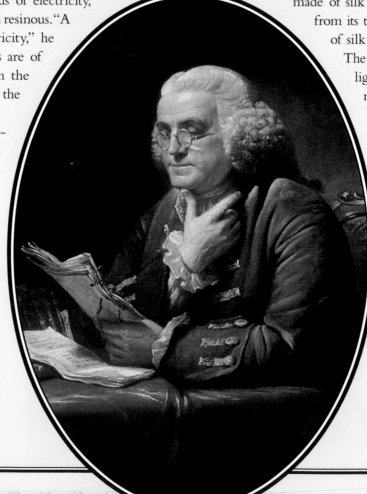

French admiration for Benjamin Franklin reached its zenith after the Revolutionary War, when it was said that he "snatched the lightning from the sky, and the scepter from the tyrants."

ity, such as the one he presented to the French court in the mid-1740s. The physicist lined up 180 policemen, linked them hand to hand, and then jolted them all with electricity that had been concentrated in a primitive condenser known as a Leyden jar.

Continuing the work of Du Fay and Nollet, Benjamin Franklin, a member of the Academy of Sciences, suggested that there was but one electricity, with positive and negative properties. However, this theory did not cause as much excitement as his 1752 kite and key experiment. In that dangerous experiment, he sent up into a thunderstorm a kite made of silk with a pointed wire projecting from its top. A key dangled from a piece of silk ribbon tied to the kite's string. The key emitted sparks, proving that lightning was an electrical phenomenon. Franklin's experiment, rejected by the British Royal Society, was reproduced by the French Academy of Sciences and the results were published in France in 1753. He went on to invent the lightning rod, which would be used to protect homes, public buildings, and even ships.

As ladies of the court look on, Abbé Nollet holds an electrified glass rod above a young man's head. When the boy is touched, sparks caused by static electricity will fly.

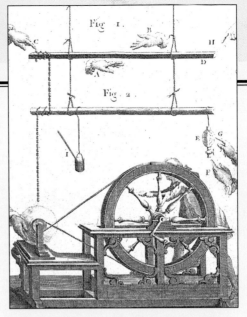

This engraving of an electricity-producing device appeared in Nollet's 1746 book, *Essay on the Electricity of the Body.*

In 1749 Nollet electrified shelves to observe the effect on the growth of plants and the appetites and health of animals.

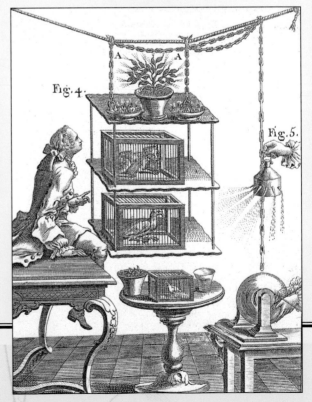

Mathematics: Science of Industry

Of all the sciences that flourished in Enlightenment France, mathematics most reflected the spirit of rationalism. When asked why he made no mention of God in his masterwork, *Celestial Mechanics,* mathematician and astronomer Pierre-Simon Laplace is said to have responded simply: "I had no need of that hypothesis."

During the age of Newton, applied mathematics was widely used in the fields of astronomy, geography and cartography, navigation, and surveying. New analytical mathematical theories were directed at and had a hand in revolutionizing French industry, specifically in the design of ships' hulls, sails, and an-chors; optics; waterwheels and turbines; and the vibrations of musical strings and metal plates.

Joseph-Louis Lagrange, the preeminent French mathematician of his generation, began his scientific studies at the age of 19. Following in the footsteps of calculus codiscoverers Sir Isaac Newton and Gottfried Wilhelm Leibniz, Lagrange created the calculus of variations and devised new techniques of working in both differential and integral calculus. King Louis XVI was so anxious to have Lagrange join the Academy of Sciences that he provided him with quarters in the Louvre. And when Lagrange suffered one of his frequent bouts of depression, Marie-Antoinette would coax him back to work.

Lagrange survived the French Revolution, and in 1791 was placed in charge of the government-appointed committee to develop new universal weights and measures. Together with the committee's other members, he devised the revolutionary calendar, as well as the metric system of measurement—perhaps the most lasting result of France's upheaval.

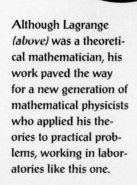

Although Lagrange *(above)* was a theoretical mathematician, his work paved the way for a new generation of mathematical physicists who applied his theories to practical problems, working in laboratories like this one.

Illustrated with landscapes and scenes of love, a calendar shows the new system put forth by Lagrange's committee. The year began at the autumnal equinox and was arranged in 12 months of 30 days, with each month containing three 10-day weeks. The months were renamed to commemorate nature and the days numbered from one to 30. Adopted by France in 1793 but not widely accepted, it was abandoned in 1806.

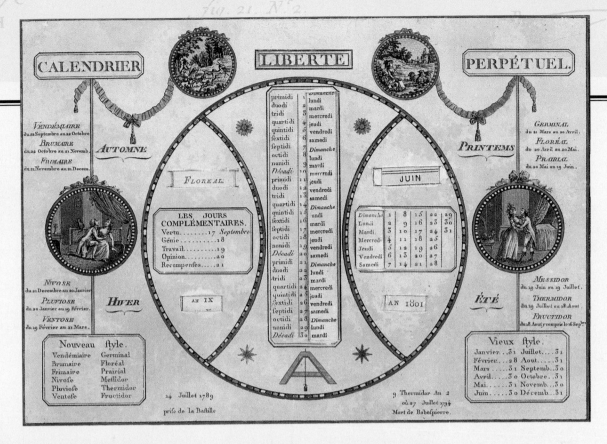

A French surveying team measures distance with an instrument called a meridian *(inset).* Lagrange's committee chose as their new unit of distance the meter, one ten-millionth of a quadrant—a quarter of the circumference of the earth.

A New Look at the Heavens

In the 17th century, Galileo's telescope opened the skies and Isaac Newton labored to devise mathematical formulas to explain the movements of the heavenly bodies. A hundred years later, the scholars of the Royal Observatory of Paris worked to improve astronomical instruments and further these discoveries, convinced that the human mind could explain and quantify all that existed in nature.

One of the finest mathematical minds at the Academy of Sciences—he submitted his first paper to them at the age of 12—was Alexis-Claude Clairaut. Clairaut began his career in 1736 as part of a French expedition to Lapland. Commissioned to measure the curvature of the earth at the Arctic Circle, the expedition returned a year later clad in furs and bringing evidence upholding Newton's theory of gravitation and claim that the earth was shaped like a sphere. Some years later, in a November 1758 presentation to the academy, Clairaut used new theories of perturbation, the effects of the attraction of a larger planet near a celestial body's path, to predict the date of the return of Halley's

Known as one of the greatest mathematical physicists in history, Laplace was quickly recognized by the Academy of Sciences, joining the group in 1773 at the age of 24.

comet. He allowed one month as a margin of error. The comet proved punctual, and Clairaut was widely declared a successor to Newton.

For all of Clairaut's success and acclaim, the second half of the 18th century belonged to mathematician and astronomer Pierre-Simon Laplace, the true giant of the age. In five papers produced between 1785 and 1788, Laplace demonstrated that the solar system was indeed stable, despite the periodic fluctuations in planetary motion observed over the centuries. Through mathematical equations, he showed that the motions of Jupiter, Saturn, and particularly the Moon were caused by the gravitational pull of the Sun and the other planets, laying to rest a question that had plagued Newton.

Laplace summed up the enormous progress made during the century in his five-volume treatise *Celestial Mechanics,* which was published between 1799 and 1825. "Astronomy, by the dignity of its object matter and the perfection of its theories," Laplace declared, "is the fairest monument of the human spirit, the noblest testimony of human intelligence."

In this 18th-century engraving, a countess is lectured on the mysteries of the heavens. The image accurately depicts astronomical discoveries of the time, including the planets orbiting the Sun, the moons of Jupiter, and Saturn's rings.

The Royal Observatory of Paris, seen below in a 17th-century print, was the center of much activity. Telescopes and meridians were set up on the grounds as well as on the roof of the observatory.

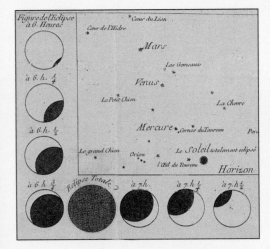

This French chart predicting the 1724 total eclipse of the Sun was given official verification "as to the time, the duration, and other respects" of the event.

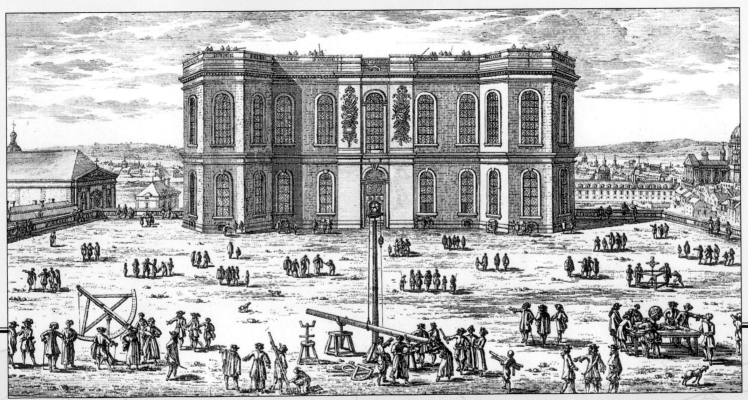

Bringing Order to Nature

While many scientists attempted to unravel the mysteries of mechanical physics and mathematics, others sought to apply those theories to living organisms. Measuring the force of muscle or describing muscular contractions did not explain the complexities of nature, however, and by the 18th century, the science of natural history was experiencing a rebirth.

Dominating this science were two bitter enemies—Swedish botanist and physician Carolus Linnaeus and French natural historian Georges-Louis Leclerc, the comte de Buffon. Linnaeus, son of a country pastor, wrote prodigiously of his botanical research, and he developed a system by which to classify all plants and animals.

He helped found the Swedish Academy of Sciences and was named a foreign correspondent of the French Academy of Sciences in 1762. Buffon, a prominent natural historian and one of the authors of the 44-volume *Histoire naturelle,* was elected to the academy in 1734, and five years later became director of the Royal Gardens in Paris.

The crux of their disagreement was Buffon's opinion that Linnaeus's system, which categorized living things in families, and then by genus and species, was based on artificial distinctions such as resemblance. Buffon's own system recognized only species—members that could produce fertile offspring together. Hostility between the two escalated to the point that Linnaeus once refused to dine in a room where Buffon's portrait was hung near his own. In the end, however, Linnaeus's system, with some modifications, prevailed.

Georges-Louis Leclerc, the comte de Buffon, and an associate wrote the most widely read scientific book in France of the 18th century. The monumental *Histoire naturelle* included the natural history of man and studies of both domesticated and wild animals.

Buffon *(seated, far left)* watches as his chief collaborator, Louis-Jean-Marie Daubenton, and a surgeon dissect a female dog during one part of a study of animal reproduction.

Buffon served for nearly 50 years as the director of the Royal Gardens, which had one of the largest collections of medicinal and ornamental plants in 18th-century Europe.

CHAPTER THREE

France to the Brink

A street market bustles outside the walls of the Châtelet courthouse and prison. The fortress was also the headquarters of the Paris police and home to an army of bureaucrats who, under the chief of police, supervised the various kinds of public works and services, from lighting streets and regulating the sale of lottery tickets to conscripting men for the militia.

 As he read the report on the desk in front of him, Paris police chief Nicolas-René Berryer allowed himself a satisfied smile. "He is an impudent character, the son of a postmaster in Péronne," stated the report on Louis-Charles Fougeret de Montbron. He was guilty of "impious talk" and "the author of an essay on sensual pleasure." Worse, Montbron wrote satires and other libels against the French government, many of which were aimed at Berryer himself. The police chief's smile broadened when he noted the report's entry for November 7 of that year, 1748: "He was arrested for having done a bad novel," it read. "The manuscript of this work was confiscated at his lodging at the time of his arrest."

Like all police reports on the writers of Paris, this one came from Berryer's inspector for the book trade, Joseph d'Hémery. It was d'Hémery's job to keep track of authors, from the highly respectable if controversial, such as Jean-Jacques Rousseau, to the most obscure—more than 400 individuals in all, or about a third of all French writers. The aim of such surveillance was to suppress any book, pamphlet, or even song that threatened to undermine public morals, the church, or the authority of the king.

From his dossiers, which contained newspaper clippings, letters, messages from police spies, and notes from interrogations at the Bastille, d'Hémery distilled reports as remarkable for their literary sensitivity as for their bureaucratic thoroughness. D'Hémery produced a virtual who's who of the French world of letters of the 18th century, full of observations and judgments. Although he was appreciative of those who showed "genius," "talent," "wit," "cleverness," and "taste," he could also be dismissive: "He writes harshly and has very little taste," he concluded about one writer; "unbearably pretentious" was his summation of another.

D'Hémery's physical descriptions of his subjects were particularly vivid, no doubt influenced by the then-popular pseudoscience of physiognomy: "fat, full-faced, and a certain something in the eyes"; "nasty, toadlike, and dying of hunger"; "swarthy, small, filthy, and disgusting"; "ill shaped, the bearing of a satyr, and a face full of pimples." Montbron he described as "tall, well built, brown complexion, and a hard physiognomy."

Assessment of a writer's personal character was his specialty. He noted of Montbron, for example, that the author had once served as a guard for the royal court "but had to give up that position because of his bad character." And of the *encyclopédiste* Denis Diderot he wrote, "He is a young man who plays the wit and prides himself on his impiety; very dangerous; speaks of the holy mysteries with scorn."

Controlling writers was just one of the myriad responsibilities of the 3,000-man department run by Nicolas Berryer, whose formal title was lieutenant general of police. Berryer had about one employee for every 200 Parisians, a much larger force in rel-

Nicknamed Monsieur Beurrier, or "Mr. Butterman," Nicolas-René Berryer became head of the capital's police in 1747 at the age of 44. Before his job as police chief, he served as intendant, or royal administrator, of Poitou, a province in west-central France.

ative terms than in most major American cities today; and given the tasks performed by his officers, he needed every one of them. Berryer's men patrolled the streets, maintained the city's prisons, fought fires, regulated commerce, set prices, controlled the city's militia, supervised the safety of buildings, handled passports, kept track of hordes of potentially suspicious folk such as foreigners, and even provided wet nurses for foundling infants. In short, the police were responsible, averred a contemporary dictionary, "for all that affects the security and comfort of the inhabitants."

Berryer had been reminded of another police responsibility that morning while making his way to work: keeping the streets of Paris clean. As usual at that time of day, the city's streets stank with accumulated garbage and trash, and a few blocks away Berryer had heard the clanging sound of hand bells. The bells were being rung by police employees who regularly walked through the neighborhoods of Paris to alert residents to pile up their waste and trash for the garbage collectors. Before he reached his office, Berryer had seen a two-wheeled horse-drawn cart roll up the street to pick up the refuse and carry it to dumps outside the city. Each cart—and there were about 130 in all that served Paris—was manned by two attendants, armed with a shovel and a broom. The attendants typically were farmers who worked land near the city and rented out their services

These prostitutes are being carted off to prison or, possibly, to the poorhouse. Although streetwalkers were considered a public menace, the police were not above recruiting them as spies.

For a small fee, a pedestrian is carried across a flooded gutter that runs down the center of a Paris street. Designed to drain off wastewater from houses, gutters frequently became so clogged with rubbish and dung that during heavy downpours they were unable to carry rainwater away.

as well as their plow horses to pull the garbage carts.

At night, Berryer's men were charged with keeping these same streets well lit. Paris had about 6,500 glass lanterns containing candles; suspended about 15 feet above the street and spaced at 45-foot intervals, they were tended by some 435 lamplighters, each of whom was assigned to no more than 15 lanterns. Thus when light-up time arrived—again signaled by policemen ringing bells—the entire city could be illuminated within half an hour. The candles in the lanterns usually guttered out around 2:00 a.m., but by then they had provided enough illumination to deter crime for the better part of the night.

Today, Berryer noted, closing the report on Montbron, was a Friday, a busy day for the lieutenant general of police. After a morning of meetings and paperwork, he prepared himself for cleaning up the city in another sense. Every Friday afternoon, between three and six o'clock, he was required to serve as a magistrate at the Châtelet, busiest of the capital's royal courts. Here he sat in judgment on a wide variety of cases, as many as 200 in a single session. Most of the cases were mundane: a guild member accused of violating the provisions of his group's charter; a surgeon whose clothes and wig had been ruined when another man spilled wine on him; a storekeeper who had failed to lock up at night as the law required; a tavern owner who'd served alcohol after 10:00 at night; parents who had defaulted on payments to a wet nurse in their employ; a citizen accused of pouring urine from an upper-story window onto the street below; three grocers charged with selling butter above the established price.

It was all routine for Berryer. But two days after his session at the Châtelet, he was expected to attend a court of a very different sort. On Sunday mornings the lieutenant of police made his weekly report to his political masters at the court of Versailles.

As his carriage traveled west out of the city toward the palace, Berryer may well have passed wagons moving in the opposite direction, laden with women. The women were wet nurses recruited by the Paris police to take care of foundlings. Every year the police took custody of about 4,000 newborn infants abandoned on the capital's streets or on church steps. To provide mother's milk for them, police employees circulated

In this 18th-century engraving, wheat, wood, and
hay from the provinces are being off-loaded on the
banks of the Seine. Food and fuel shortages often
led to civil disturbances in the capital.

Some of the packages of books sitting outside this bookstore in Liège, Belgium, are probably destined for France. To circumvent state censors, French writers often published their books abroad and had them smuggled back across the border.

THE WORLD OF PRINT

While they may not have been members of the exalted republic of letters or may not have attended the literary salons of Paris, millions of ordinary Frenchmen and -women of the 18th century were avid readers. Literacy rates had increased steadily during the century—reaching as high as 47 percent for men and 27 percent for women—and the increased demand for reading materials had caused an explosion in the world of print.

Periodicals containing sensational political gossip and scandal made up the bulk of what was produced. But the public also read books on philosophy and the arts and sciences. Diderot's *Encyclopédie,* Buffon's *Histoire naturelle,* and Voltaire's collected works, for example, sold well. In fiction, the novel debuted and proved immensely popular. Readers craved stories about people confronting life's troubles and tales of virtuous yet distressed heroines saved in the end by either marriage or death. Fictional travel memoirs were another popular genre that allowed writers to weave political and social criticism into entertaining stories of exotic peoples and places. And although books remained expensive, the majority of them could be borrowed at the lending libraries—an invention of the 18th century—that sprang up in cities and provincial centers throughout the country.

Whether for instruction or entertainment, books were treasured possessions during the Enlightenment. At right, a schoolboy studies his lessons, and above, young ladies and gentlemen gather in a library to read and converse.

through the villages surrounding Paris to find wet nurses. Women willing to breast-feed a second or third child for money were transported to Paris, matched up with foundlings, and then returned to their homes. But even with the best efforts of the police and the surrogate mothers, mortality rates were high: More than 30 percent of the infants taken into care failed to survive their first year.

Looking after foundlings was just one aspect of the police department's social-welfare program for the residents of Paris. Using funds provided by the Crown, the church, and various private sources, the police also tried to head off the food shortages that could so often lead to rioting. In times of hardship they distributed rice, fish, and coal to the poor, found jobs for the out of work, and even provided small monthly allowances for the particularly needy. And now that December was almost here, Berryer knew he would have to dispatch agents to the provinces to find the additional quantities of grain, vegetables, and fish that Parisians would consume during the meatless Lent.

Reflecting on a police chief's unique vantage point on the

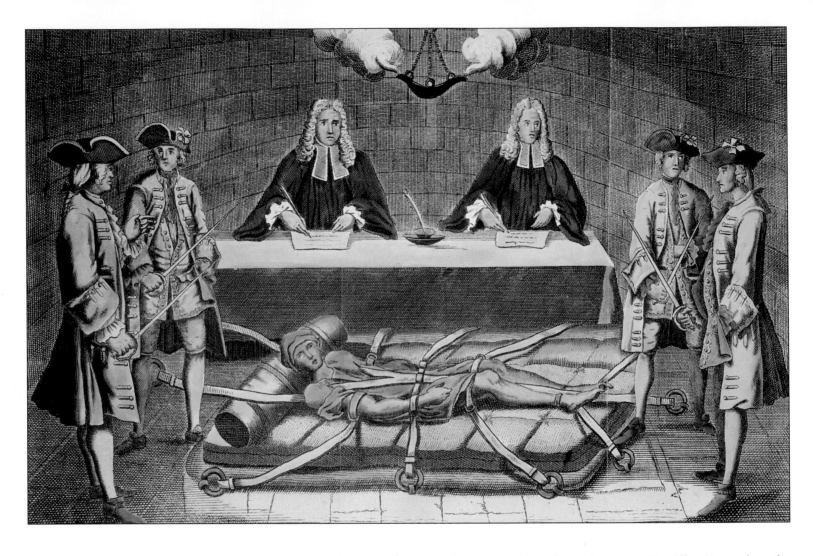

THE PRICE OF REGICIDE

On January 5, 1757, a domestic servant named Robert-François Damiens was arrested after an unsuccessful attempt to assassinate Louis XV. Fearing a conspiracy, the police put the would-be assassin to "the question": His legs were bound tightly together *(above)*, his knees and ankles were forced apart by wooden wedges driven between them, and four gallons of water were poured down his throat. But Damiens named no coconspirators. Finally, he was tied hand and foot to four powerful horses that pulled in opposite directions until his limbs separated from his torso.

extremes within French society, Berryer continued on his way to Versailles. Few others, he mused, had the opportunity to touch both the squalor of the kingdom and the magnificence of the royal court. And at that court few enjoyed the enviable status of the lieutenant general of police.

As the principal instrument of the king's will in the capital, Berryer enjoyed enormous power and prestige, and was addressed as Monseigneur, a title normally reserved for bishops or members of the royal family. During his weekly visits to Versailles, he conferred with the king's ministers or, on occasion, with King Louis XV himself. His power was further amplified by his status as a protégé of the king's official mistress, Madame de Pompadour, who had secured the job for Berryer in 1747, when he was 44 years old and working as a lawyer. According to a contemporary, Berryer was her "confidential agent, her 'creature' in all respects."

Both Pompadour and Louis considered the police the best means of stamping out sedition, and Berryer, accordingly, devoted much of his energies to the surveillance of the population of Paris. Part of this surveillance was carried out by the approximately 1,500 blue-uniformed men who patrolled the city streets on foot or on horseback. They alone among Paris's citizenry were authorized to bear firearms. Berryer also commanded a plainclothes force. The core of this force was a group of 20 or more inspectors who examined the daily registers of hotels and boardinghouses, visited the shops and stalls of merchants of secondhand goods to look for stolen articles, checked the reports of doctors and surgeons who had treated wounds, and perused the records of midwives detailing the babies they had delivered.

Keeping an eye on everything required an additional clandestine force of nearly 1,000 full- and part-time informers. Parisians were convinced that such informers were everywhere, and the police did all they could to encourage this belief. The inspectors called them subinspectors or undercover agents; the people referred to them as *mouches*—"flies." Most were recruited from the lowest levels of society, even from prison, and they were universally detested and distrusted. It was these mouches who prowled the inns and restaurants during Lent to make sure only the sick and pregnant ate meat. On Sundays they prevented all commerce except the sale of food, and they even monitored churchgoers to make certain that their behavior and dress were sufficiently solemn.

A favorite venue of the police spy was the tavern. The lower classes of Paris—women as well as men—frequented the neighborhood tavern to eat, drink wine, socialize, and play games like billiards, chess, darts, dice, and cards. People found jobs in the taverns and transacted business there. The tavern also was the scene of much that interested the police: brawls, prostitution, seditious talk, the fencing of stolen goods. "Let the Parisian popular classes off the leash," warned the writer and social critic Louis-

Sébastien Mercier, and "there would be no holding them back; released from their accustomed control [by the police], the populace would give way to violence which would be all the more cruel because they themselves would not know where to stop."

Berryer waged a campaign to keep prostitutes out of the taverns and off the streets. Though prostitution was technically illegal, he agreed to tolerate it if the women practiced their trade in carefully regulated brothels. Brothel keepers had to make certain their recruits were experienced sexually and not virgins by presenting them to the appropriate police inspector for examination. They also were required to file weekly reports on their customers. Names of prominent persons furnished police with the possibility of blackmail or political leverage. Berryer learned, for example, that the pope's minister in France, the papal nuncio, had become so attached to a prostitute at Madame Baudouin's brothel that the young woman—who became pregnant—visited him twice a week at his residence and led him "to believe that the pregnancy is his doing."

Among the chief targets of Berryer's spies were migrants from the French countryside. The migrants were easy to spot; unlike longtime residents, who tended to be plump and pale, the newcomers were generally lean and tanned from hours of hard labor in the sun, their clothes ragged and dirty. Some two-thirds of those who appeared before the city's courts hailed from outside of Paris. Many ended up as vagrants, vagabonds, and beggars, and hundreds of officers were assigned the task of keeping them off the streets.

Berryer's determination to round up vagrants was intensified by a new royal edict in November 1749. Famine in the countryside had driven an unusually large number of starving people into Paris; by the following year the city would have an estimated 15,000 beggars. "His Majesty commands that all beggars and vagrants found in the streets of Paris," the edict directed, "of whatever age or sex, shall be arrested and taken to prison." Taking literally the stipulation about age, Berryer ordered a crackdown on the young, especially on those found gambling in the streets or roaming the city in gangs. He offered a bounty for each young vagrant arrested, announcing, "I only part with money when the goods are delivered."

Soon, teenagers and even younger children began disappearing from the streets. Policemen in plain clothes would approach a group of youngsters and then whisk them off to prison in closed carriages, bypassing the usual arrest procedure in which a suspect was taken before a district police commissioner to determine if action was warranted. Eager to augment their meager incomes with the promised bounty, the police acted indiscriminately, collecting not just vagrant children but the offspring of respectable merchants and tradesmen. Many of the youths themselves had jobs as apprentices or clerks. Berryer did not object to the wide net his men were casting. He explained that for months he'd been receiving complaints from parents about their delinquent children stealing money from them in order to gamble openly in the public squares. Such parents, he said, actually wanted their children to be arrested to chasten them and set an example for others.

But by May 1750, when several hundred children had been abducted, the women of Paris were up in arms. Berryer became a target of invective, in part because of his connection to Madame de Pompadour, who was known in the taverns as the "king's whore." Wild rumors began to spread. One story had it that the children were being transported to North America to populate the French colonies there; wilder tales told of children being bled to death to provide a blood-bath cure for a leprous prince or princess or, in one version, the king himself. Women drew up petitions against the arbitrary arrests and complained to the police commissioners in their districts. When the arrests continued, the concern and anger in the streets boiled over. On May 16 a mother holding her child by the hand grew suspicious of a passing carriage laden with policemen. Tightening her hold on the child, she loudly called attention to the vehicle, and a crowd swarmed over the carriage, attacking the policemen. One person was killed and several were injured.

A dead cat dangles from a pole during this 1768 riot in Lyon sparked by a rumor that infants were being abducted and used for anatomy experiments. Violence was commonplace in 18th-century France, especially among the young and the poor. Brawls and riots erupted frequently, often over minor insults, new taxes, and the mere hint of famine.

AD OPERAM.

ANGÉLIQUE MARGUERITE DUCOUDRAY.

Pensionnée et envoyée par le Roy, pour enseigner à pratiquer l'art des Accouchements dans tout le Royaume.

Gravé par J. Robert.

Midwife Madame du Coudray, shown here in her book on childbirth, was asked by Louis XV to teach peasant girls how to deliver babies safely. Du Coudray's efforts contributed to an upswing in the population.

A week later, violence erupted throughout the city. On May 22 confrontations with constables took place in six different parts of Paris. At the slightest provocation, crowds of hundreds and sometimes thousands attacked the police with fists, sticks, and stones and ransacked shops for weapons. The protesters were a cross section of people—women, merchants, and artisans as well as vagrants and troublemakers. An estimated 20 of them were killed in the melees.

Trouble flared again the following day in the parish of Saint-Roch on the Right Bank of the Seine between the Palais Royal and the Saint-Honoré market. That morning around nine o'clock a plain-clothes constable named Labbé was spotted trying to arrest an 11-year-old boy. In response, a group of citizens rushed in to free the child and attack the policeman. Labbé, although injured, fled into the market. His pursuers saw him run through the stalls and then dart into a building overlooking the market; the building, on the Rue Bout du Monde, was home to his mistress, a laundress who worked as a police spy. Labbé was cornered. Found in an attic room, hiding under a bed, he was dragged downstairs and out into the street.

Only the arrival of the police saved Labbé from a lynching. Rescuing their colleague from the clutches of the growing mob, the officers accompanied him to the residence of a police commissioner in the Rue Saint-Honoré, which was nearby. The crowd followed, ignoring Labbé's protests that he was only "a simple wine merchant's lad," a claim he tried to back up by waving a corkscrew in the air.

When Labbé was taken inside the commissioner's house, the protesters tried to follow. A group of police officers attempted to hold them at bay with bayonets. Someone in the mob fired a pistol, shots were exchanged, and the people forced their way into the house. Labbé was seized. Though he managed to break away from the mob one more time, he was recaptured outside the church of Saint-Roch, where he was beaten and stoned to death.

The rioters were still not finished. Next they dragged Labbé's corpse to the residence of the man responsible for the child abductions: the lieutenant general of police, Nicolas Berryer. But before they could lay siege to the house, Berryer eluded them by sneaking through his garden and making his escape. A large group of policemen then arrived, several of whom retrieved Labbé's body and carried it to the morgue on a ladder.

The following night, a small group of people gathered in the Rue Bout du Monde outside the home of Labbé's mistress. In the street under her windows they lit a fire and staged a mock religious ceremony. Someone slit the throat of a cat. The carcass was blessed with "holy water" from the gutter and then, while hymns were sung, flung into the flames. The crowd jeered and shouted threats that all police spies would suffer the same fate.

increasing grip of the police, the parlement, and the king. Thereafter, Louis XV and Madame de Pompadour—more hated than ever—avoided traversing the streets of Paris.

Although Nicolas Berryer's implementation of the king's will had penalized the capital's children, another of the king's servants intended only to improve the lives of the children of France. Her name was Madame du Coudray, and as the king's official midwife, she found herself on the road again, those rutted and rocky byways of provincial France far from her native Paris. Her stagecoach, drawn by four horses, lurched to and fro as it picked its way past the creaking farm wagons, heavily laden donkeys, and flocks of sheep that periodically brought all forward progress to a

"What number of children [are] dead or maimed by the negligence of their wet nurses?"

A judicial inquiry was eventually called to investigate the whole affair of the disappearing children of Paris. Berryer was given a tacit rebuke: He was ordered to clean up his methods and make certain his men adhered to the standard procedure of taking suspects to the nearest commissioner in order to determine whether legal proceedings should be initiated. Four policemen were ordered to pay small fines and forced to kneel for their reprimands in the Great Hall of Parlement, the sovereign law court. The rioters certainly got the worst of it, however. Three of them were hanged for their roles in the violence. Yet during the executions in the Place de Grève on August 3, the people made one last show of defiance, surging forward until soldiers pushed them back at bayonet point. Like the riots over the vanishing children, it was a spasm of protest against the ever-

halt. The dusty roads were filled with people too, most of them members of the *population flottante,* the "floating population"— the hundreds of thousands of peasants who could no longer make a living from the land and now drifted permanently about the countryside, scavenging food and stealing.

Madame du Coudray took little notice. This 48-year-old woman, her ample proportions well cushioned against the jolting ride, was accustomed to life on the road—and extremely single minded. She was a woman with a mission. King Louis XV believed that the population of France was shrinking, and he had commissioned her to spur the nation's demographic revival by reducing infant mortality: It was Madame du Coudray's job to teach poor, untrained women of the countryside how to safely deliver babies. Her destination on this day in the late spring of

1763 was Limoges, the capital city of Limousin, a remote and backward province in central France.

As she rode, du Coudray could be forgiven if she reminisced about how far she had progressed. Her real name was Angélique Marguerite Le Boursier, and she did not talk freely of her origins, which would always remain a mystery; there was speculation that she might even have begun life as an abandoned child. As far as the historical record is concerned, her story begins in 1740, when she completed the three-year apprenticeship required of midwives in Paris, passed the required examinations of the College of Surgery, and then waited five months while the police compiled the necessary interviews with her parish priest and other character references. Over the next decade she taught apprentices of her own while annually delivering as many as 100 infants in Paris. She was also developing influential friends.

One of those friends, the well-connected maverick surgeon and monk Frère Côme, became her principal supporter. Largely because of Côme, her life underwent a radical change. In 1751, upon Côme's enthusiastic recommendation, she was hired by a wealthy philanthropist to teach the techniques of childbirth to the peasant women living on his estates in Auvergne.

In this southern province the midwife encountered for the first time the brutish reality of life in the French countryside. Most peasants there went hungry, subsisting mainly on a bread-and-water porridge augmented occasionally with vegetables grown on small plots and chestnuts and berries gathered from the forests. They rarely ate meat. Men scratched a meager living from the land using primitive plows little different from those of the ancient Romans. Caught in a vicious cycle, they could not raise

Although rural life appears quaint in this 1786 painting, most French peasants were chronically poor and malnourished, sometimes forced to eat the seed needed for the next year's planting.

enough grain to feed livestock and not enough livestock to produce manure to fertilize the fields and increase grain yields. What little they could harvest was undercut by rents and taxes.

Birth in the countryside was thus not always a joyous event. It meant a new mouth to feed, and frequently the burden of the additional child was sufficient to uproot the family and send them on the road as part of the population flottante. To decrease the number of children they bore, peasant women tended to marry late, in their mid-20s. This shortened period of fertility helped limit the size of the family to perhaps only a half-dozen children, of whom fewer than half were likely to survive to adulthood. It has been estimated that at least 45 percent of those born in France during the 1700s died before the age of 10.

The midwife from Paris also saw firsthand how ignorance contributed to this dismal record. Supervision of birthing in the countryside typically was entrusted to experienced but untrained village matrons who practiced the traditional—and often tragic—ways. In the process of "making new feet," as delivery was known, such matters as the careful coiffuring of the mother's hair, which was believed to bring about a favorable outcome, took precedence over hygiene and safe technique. The matron might render the infant blind with a jagged dirty fingernail or cause brain damage by attempting to reshape the malleable head into a more pleasing shape. If the birth went slowly, she might encourage the mother to jump to dislodge the baby; in some regions the custom was to walk around once the baby's head appeared, a practice that frequently resulted in strangulation.

In Auvergne, where she soon was giving free lessons under the sponsorship of the provincial government, du Coudray wrote a birthing textbook, *Abridgment of the Art of Delivery*. It was a practical, how-to manual, with anatomical drawings that attempted to dispel the aura of superstition surrounding childbirth and frame the event instead as a mechanical problem that had to be solved. But since few of her country students could read, the book wound up serving as a kind of marketing tool among the educated elite. It received favorable reviews in the press and enhanced Du Coudray's professional status among the medical men and bureaucrats she needed to impress.

Her primary teaching tool was the obstetrical mannequin she invented in 1756 to enable her to simulate live births. It would make her lessons "understood by minds unaccustomed to grasping things except through the senses." The malleable mannequin, fashioned out of buff-colored linen, soft leather, stuffing, and actual human bones, represented a life-size woman complete with a womb and other organs, all conveniently numbered. A baby doll was attached by umbilical cord. The student could maneuver the flexible doll, delivering it from every conceivable position and presentation, and thus prepare for all eventualities. Madame du Coudray called her mannequin a "machine," a name that exemplified the Enlightenment love of automatons.

Her teaching work in Auvergne, together with her machine and textbook, coincided with the king's concern about depopulation. In 1759, France was in the midst of the fighting that came to be known as the Seven Years' War, and the government was obsessed with the need for soldiers. The king, hoping that this remarkable midwife could make sure more healthy babies were born, issued a royal brevet, or commission, mobilizing the nation in a fight against infant mortality. He ordered that she was to enjoy royal patronage and protection, traveling freely on a nationwide teaching mission "without encountering, for any reason, trouble from any person or under any pretext whatsoever."

When she arrived in Limoges in the spring of 1763, she came with the highest endorsements. "The infinite good she has brought has far surpassed our hopes," wrote the intendant of Bourbonnais, one of 30 provincial administrators appointed by the king. Along the way, she had become Madame du Coudray, a name she had taken, with its false implications that she was mar-

THE ART OF DELIVERY

The color illustrations below are taken from Madame du Coudray's book, *Abridgment of the Art of Delivery*. Du Coudray hoped that the pictures would, as she put it, "remind my students of my own demonstrations," which she performed with an obstetrical mannequin. At top, the pelvic anatomy is depicted, along with an infant in utero; below, a midwife's white-cuffed hands correctly *(left)* and incorrectly *(right)* deliver breech babies.

The book had a threefold purpose. While its illustrations would help the mostly illiterate young women she'd coached in childbirth procedures, the book's clear instructions would provide other readers with a how-to manual more practical than existing medical texts. The book also was an effective marketing tool, a ticket that du Coudray gave to intendants to gain entrée to teach in their regions.

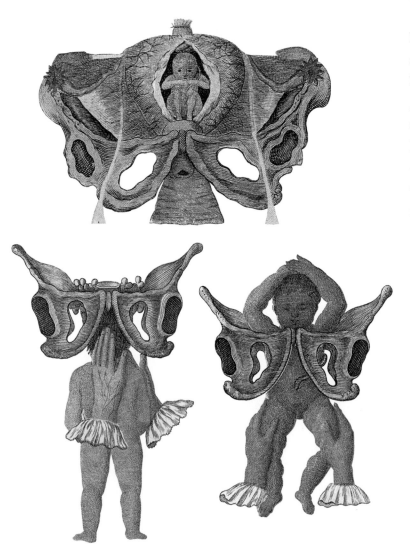

ried and of noble birth, in order to ease her travels among men.

She had spent nearly three years on the road and perfected a routine. Her course lasted two months and was bracketed by rest periods of two weeks before and after. The province or community paid her 300 livres a month and purchased several mannequins at 300 livres each. The course usually took place in the *hôtel de ville,* or town hall. Du Coudray was provided with transportation, lodging, wood for heating, candles, and household utensils. In these days she still traveled alone, but later her hosts would need to provide a house for an entourage of up to five, including a chambermaid, cook, and male servant.

By all accounts, du Coudray got along well with her host in Limoges. Anne-Robert-Jacques Turgot was the energetic intendant for the province of Limousin, and he shared du Coudray's humanitarian concern for the poor. Turgot, an up-and-coming 36-year-old reformer who would later become finance minister of France, was doing his best to bring change to the province. He was improving the roads and bridges and easing the tax burden on the poor. He was also attempting to promote a new food, the potato, to supplement the sparse local grain crops, but he was running into resistance from the conservative peasants. "In the Limousin," he wrote in despair, "there are hardly any peasants who can read or write, and very few upon whom one can count for intelligence or probity; they are a stubborn race, opposing even changes which are designed for their own good."

Recruitment of students—*"mes femmes,"* as du Coudray called them—went slowly for the course in Limoges, an old city of around 14,000 inhabitants, most of whom lived in mud-wall houses. As elsewhere in the provinces, many of the young women who were potential students found it difficult to be available for the required two months. The community or church typically paid to support them during the course, and priests were asked to select candidates for their alertness and youth. But their families were loath to spare them for so long a time. They were indispensable on their little family farms, performing every chore, from helping to spread manure and plowing to hauling water, milking the cows, cooking, sewing, scrubbing, and looking after the younger children.

Both teacher and provincial chief were disappointed by the turnout in Limoges, which fell far short of the normal enrollment of 70 to 80 students. Turgot castigated his underlings for not doing a better job of advertising the course. When du Coudray moved in November to the nearby town of Tulle, which was smaller and even more notorious for its conservatism and frugality, Turgot offered an incentive for students. He promised they would be exempt from taxation on all their future earnings as midwives. For his own political future as well as the good of the town, he wanted the course to succeed.

To the barefoot peasant girls who attended, the course must have seemed like a wondrous theatrical performance. The cloth mannequins and anatomical posters resembled a theatrical set; and Madame du Coudray, her double chin held high, was the star performer. The course consisted of about 40 daylong lessons. Du Coudray began by reminding her students of their duty as midwives to serve all women no matter how poor and no matter what their marital status. She then moved on to practical lessons in basic anatomy and physiology. In keeping with medical practice of the day, she emphasized the need to bleed pregnant women from leg, arm, and neck at regular intervals to get rid of surplus bodily fluids. Then she had each of the students practice extensively on the machine, learning to perform "all the deliveries imaginable," as du Coudray put it.

The course concluded with advice aimed at placating the institutions she had to keep on her side: the medical establishment, the church, and the state. She took pains to describe and demonstrate the emergency conditions under which a surgeon or doctor must be called in. She emphasized the necessity of baptism. The midwife herself must perform this act—even reaching in with a syringe, if necessary—when the infant's survival appeared unlikely. Otherwise, as soon as the mother was strong enough to make the trip, the midwife would make arrangements with the priest and then carry the newborn to church in the traditional large baptismal cloth of muslin and lace.

Finally, mindful of her obligation to the state and her mission to help boost France's population, du Coudray cautioned her students to take care in the selection of wet nurses if they were required. Many wet nurses, she pointed out, offered their services only because they were poverty stricken, and they frequently suffered from inadequate nutrition and sanitation. Many of them exercised poor judgment by taking children into the bed with them, and so risked smothering them. "What number of children [are] dead or maimed by the negligence of their wet nurses?" she asked rhetorically. "It is indeed shameful that the state loses so many subjects." By saving these "treasures of great price," she said, her students would enrich the nation.

Afterward, the intendant Turgot praised du Coudray highly. However, he also admitted that he had been taken aback somewhat by her imperious manner. Her work, he wrote to the intendant of Bordeaux, was "extremely useful" and the costs of the course money "well spent." But he could not resist the chance to point out "the high estimation she has of herself." Another provincial official put it more bluntly when he spoke of "her unendurable arrogance."

Part of the problem was that men in official positions were not accustomed to a strong, capable woman who proclaimed her own worth. But du Coudray also was in fact a shameless self-promoter who spoke of her calling as the "good of humanity" and her textbook and mannequin as "monuments to posterity for centuries to come." She must have felt she had to be pushy in order to maintain her extraordinary mission through all the vicissitudes of policy and personnel change at Versailles. It was not enough just to be a good teacher. She had to collect enthu-

HEALING THE SICK

Medicine," declared a French physician of the 1740s, "is a commodity that everyone wants." Judging by the astonishing range of health-promoting elixirs, powders, instruments, and therapies advertised in the newspapers of the day, he was right. Fortifying one's health had become especially fashionable in Paris. There the well-to-do eagerly purchased any product that was labeled as *de santé,* or "healthful," while the state promoted a number of public-health initiatives, such as the eradication of stench—which was thought to be an indicator of the presence of disease—and improvements in the city's water supply.

Popular enthusiasm for preventive medicine reflected a confidence in humanity's ability to improve the mortal condition. Indeed, it was during the 18th century that inoculation against smallpox was first developed. But in an era when any illness—as well as many "cures"—could prove lethal, even the uneducated realized the advantages of staying healthy. Throughout the 1700s, treatments remained rudimentary. The basic prescription, whether for typhus or gout, was to rid the body of toxins through bloodletting, purges, and enemas, then allow the body to heal itself with sleep, exercise, air, and a restorative diet. Recuperation, physicians counseled, should take place in the country, where the air was cleaner, or by taking the waters at a natural spa.

Whereas physicians specialized in the treatment of disease, the setting of bones and the dressing of wounds were left to surgeons.

Studying a urine sample, a physician tries to diagnose a young woman's ailment while family members crowd round.

Although it was still regarded as "the cutter's art," surgery had become more reputable in 18th-century France, where the surgeons were among the best in all of Europe. But surgery continued to be thought of as a lowly calling, and many practicing surgeons had little training and often began their careers as barbers. A surgical caseload typically included such duties as lancing boils, dressing skin infections, pulling teeth, supervising difficult births, and amputating limbs, all of which were performed without the aid of anesthetics or antiseptics. Not surprisingly, Diderot's *Encyclopédie* warned patients to undergo surgery only as a last resort.

An alternative to licensed medicine was the practice of folk medicine. Reflecting the growing reliance on science, trained medical men had nothing but disdain for such traditional methods or for those who practiced them. "Our towns and rural areas," complained one city doctor in 1772, "are populated by old bedside watchers who imagine that because they have handed out some bouillons they can exercise the full extent of medicine. . . . Poisons, blades, and daggers are less dangerous than their remedies." But ordinary people were not so sure. Trained doctors were readily available only in the larger cities, where they concentrated on taking care of the wealthy. Elsewhere, local herbalists and folk healers were often easier to find in times of need than the formally trained—and highly priced—men of medicine.

Armed with a most intimidating syringe, a physician approaches a bedridden patient to administer an enema.

A lady's arm is prepared for bloodletting— also known as "breathing a vein"—in the hope that this would clear her body of contaminated blood.

siastic endorsements from the provincial intendants everywhere she went and keep reminding all who would listen of the uniqueness of her assignment. "My zeal," she once wrote, "showed me the way."

All the same, du Coudray went out of her way to be solicitous of surgeons and doctors, who might well regard her as a trespasser upon medical turf. She was at pains to not appear to be "passing myself off as a Doctor." Whatever her true feelings, she avoided the kind of antimale rhetoric espoused by Elizabeth Nihell, the controversial English midwife. Like du Coudray, Nihell had trained in Paris and published a book on midwifery. But Nihell's book was an impassioned attack on male surgeons who delivered babies. Women were far better suited for the task, she maintained, possessed as they were of a "supremely tender sensibility."

Du Coudray and other French midwives were caught in the cross fire between surgeons and doctors. In the early 18th century surgeons had been professionally associated with barbers and wigmakers—surgeons even gave shaves. But the king's patronage had elevated them to the plateau of prestige occupied by their bitter rivals, the doctors. Now surgeons were intruding upon the domain not only of doctors but of midwives as well; through their influence, midwives were prevented from forming their own pro-

A corpse draws the attention of medical students attending an anatomy lecture at the Paris School of Surgery.

fessional guild and were even barred from utilizing the newest techniques and instruments of the obstetrical trade.

In 1766, three years after her courses in Limousin, du Coudray must have taken enormous satisfaction when she was invited to teach obstetrics to the surgeons of His Majesty's navy, many of whom would perform such duties in the colonies. She conducted the course in the city of Rochefort, an important maritime center on the Atlantic coast. In her lessons she emphasized the use of Cesarean sections and forceps, the very tools and techniques forbidden to midwives. To make her demonstrations even

The window frames built in the carpentry workshop above will go to a glazier to be fitted with glass panes. By the early 1700s cloth and oilpaper windows were giving way to glass, which greatly improved the lighting and heating of buildings.

more realistic for the navy surgeons, she equipped her mannequin with an elaborate set of sponges saturated with clear and opaque red fluids to simulate the action of blood and amniotic fluid. Eleven of her students were so impressed by her knowledge and teaching techniques that they composed an official letter of appreciation: "She rightly deserves the brilliant praises that are won for her everywhere by her great reputation."

Teaching the surgeons was a crowning moment for du Coudray, but it barely paid her expenses. The fees for her courses, together with profits from selling textbooks and mannequins, provided just enough to get by. For years she had hoped for a royal pension—an annual salary from the government—only to be disappointed. One government plan proposed that each province

In the early 1760s, when Madame du Coudray was launching her remarkable mission to rural France, she may have unknowingly crossed paths with another peripatetic Parisian. Jacques-Louis Ménétra was half her age and made no pretensions to noble status or saving humanity. Instead of riding with dignity in a stagecoach, he walked from town to town with a bold and confident stride, offering his services as a glazier. He wore a jerkin and leather trousers, and his glazier's apron was rolled up and slung across his chest as a bandolier to conceal the pistol he carried for protection against bandits and wolves. The bag slung over his back contained everything he owned—most important, the hammer, nails, and diamond glass cutter that were the tools of his trade.

Ménétra was in the midst of his *tour de*

"Getting ahead was her main passion, and mine was to enjoy myself."

contribute to a fund for her annual payment, but an incipient rebellion against royal authority caused this scheme to fail.

Then, in August 1767, came a new royal brevet for Madame du Coudray. "His Majesty wants and ordains that, as long as she gives public courses of instruction anywhere in the realm, she enjoy, each year, the sum of 8,000 livres." A pension for retirement—later increased to the same amount—was also ordained. By the time she stopped traveling in the early 1780s at the age of 67, she had taught in more than 40 cities all across France, helping to train an estimated 10,000 students. Thanks to improved public health, increased agricultural production, and the skill and persistence of this extraordinary woman of the Enlightenment, the population of France—of such concern to the king—was no longer shrinking.

France, a traditional rite of passage for young artisans. In order to perfect their craft and earn status as master guildsmen, all sorts of artisans, from glaziers and carpenters to cobblers and locksmiths, spent years traveling and working around the country. Ménétra in his seven years on the road would trek some 1,600 miles, much of it in southern France, stopping off for lengthy periods in cities where the work or play appealed to him. Under the supervision of the master glaziers who employed him in the provinces, he learned to install the new large glass panels that were just coming into vogue, as well as the traditional small panes. He fashioned lanterns for street lighting, installed glass in the king's ships, and repaired elaborate stained-glass windows in convents and castles.

But the aspiring artisan's tour de France was about learning to live as well as work. Ménétra and others like him went on the road to break free from home and accomplish the transition from adolescence to the responsibilities of adult life. Among his fellows, a free-spirited group, Ménétra stood out. He was small in stature but possessed an enormous appetite for having a good time—for drinking and joking with his comrades and seducing women. These were the "years of pleasure," he would write afterward of his touring period. "And each year was a century of happiness."

Like most French artisans of the day, Ménétra was born into his trade. Put out to a wet nurse at birth, he lost his mother before he was two years old, and his maternal grandmother took him in after she discovered that his most recent wet nurse had taught him to beg outside a church, mimicking her own foster child. He apprenticed under his father, who had his own shop, and his mother's four brothers, who were all glaziers. The relationship with his father was complex and stormy. The senior Ménétra cared enough to join with neighbors in forming an escort to protect their children on their way home from school during the notorious police kidnappings in 1750, when the boy was 11. But the father was given to drink and outbursts of temper. On one occasion, he

Economist, reformer, administrator, and statesman Anne-Robert-Jacques Turgot was bound for the priesthood before he decided to dedicate himself to public service and the employ of his king. During his 13 years as royal administrator in Limousin, he built more than 400 miles of roads, similar to the cobblestoned highway at right, and tried to modernize agricultural practice in this backward French province.

LOUIS'S RADICAL REFORMER

Despite their position as defenders of the established order, the kings of France tried some reforms. In fact, when appointing officers of the Crown, they often chose progressive, liberal-minded men who put the common good above narrower interests. The most enlightened of these public servants was Anne-Robert-Jacques Turgot.

Turgot rose to prominence during his service as provincial intendant of Limousin, where his modern methods so impressed the philosophes that they became convinced he alone could save the country from its political and financial malaise. Partly as a result of their lobbying, Turgot was appointed minister of finance in 1774 to the newly anointed Louis XVI.

As finance minister, Turgot abolished the corvée system of forced peasant labor and established free trade in grain sales. He proposed a new civil-law code to ensure religious toleration for French Protestants, tried to impose taxes on the clergy, and developed plans for local self-government. But the opposition forces were too great. In the end, even Turgot's zeal could do little to move the vested interests of the day—or to save the man in whose name he tried to change France, King Louis XVI.

dislocated his son's leg; on another he broke his jaw and knocked out teeth.

Young Jacques was glad to get away. He was 18 in March 1757 when he began his tour de France, having completed his four years of apprenticeship to become a *compagnon* (companion), or journeyman, a status that would require at least six more years of work before he was eligible to become a master glazier. Hundreds of other journeymen were on the road at the same time, and virtually all of them belonged to a workers' association known as a *compagnonnage*. There were three of these nationwide groups. They had been founded during the 16th century to protect the interests of workers from the power of the guild masters in the various trades. Clandestine in the beginning but no longer so in the 18th century, each group nevertheless retained its own secret rites and fierce group pride.

Ménétra was initiated into the compagnonnage around 1758, a year after he began his tour. His initiation ceremony included a requirement that he copy the statutes of the organization and compile a list of all of the companions arriving in town. This requirement reflected the high degree of literacy among the companions. Having grown up in Paris, Ménétra, like most boys there, had gone to school. Girls in Paris and both sexes in the provinces, by comparison, had much less opportunity for schooling. While on the road, Ménétra wrote letters to his grandmother back home, main-

tained the necessary commercial correspondence, and read newspapers and an occasional book. Even more surprising, he would later pen a 500-page autobiography, *Journal of My Life*.

The compagnonnage became Ménétra's surrogate family. In each city, members found lodging at an inn managed by a woman known appropriately as "mother." Together with her husband, "father," she informed members of available job opportunities and advanced them money when necessary. The brethren came together regularly to play and sometimes to fight. There were occasional pitched battles between members of rival groups in which members fought with rocks, fists, and wooden canes. Mostly they danced, ran footraces, and played tennis. They met every night at the inn to eat, drink, sing, play pranks on one another, and share stories—and sometimes women—to express their brotherhood. If a member took ill, they carried him to the hospital. If he went to jail, they visited him

and provided financial support. When he left town, they formed a bodyguard to escort him to the countryside in a ceremonial procession complete with music.

Ménétra had a good voice, a memory for the songs he had learned as a boy in choir school, and a gift for improvising tunes. One night over wine in the southeastern city of Carpentras, he made up a song about the town. The next day all the companions took off from work and took to the streets. "Violins and oboes were brought in," Ménétra recalled, "and everybody had a bottle and a glass "in hand." In front of them strode a journeyman locksmith who had the lyrics written in large letters in chalk on his back. "We sang it over and over," Ménétra reminisced in his *Journal,* pleasing "the residents who followed us from corner to corner through the town."

In three different cities, Ménétra had occasion to preside over both the fun and the serious work of the compagnonnage after he was elected for a one-year term as "first companion" by his brethren. The companions' social season peaked each year with the celebration of the feast day of the glaziers' patron saint. In Lyon the celebrations that Ménétra planned for the festival of Saint Luke on October 18, 1762, became one of the high points of his life. As first companion, he organized a week-long celebration the likes of which had rarely been seen by the local citizenry. In preparation, his brethren insisted on carrying him around in a sedan chair to make certain all the master glaziers had draped their shops with flowers. At each stop, he and his bearers partook of the proffered refreshment—so much so, he related, that his "horses" faltered and turned over the chair, tumbling their first companion ignominiously to the ground.

The festival's highlights included a ball, a banquet, and a special High Mass at the cathedral. But perhaps Ménétra's proudest moments came during the procession. Four apprentices carried an enormous holy bread baked for the occasion.

The companions were decked out in gray suits with white gloves and stockings. Their hair was curled and festooned with white ribbons. Each carried a walking stick and a bouquet. "All Lyon turned out to see us march in twos myself in the lead with two ribbons in the third buttonhole."

The lavish festival expressed the extravagance of young companions who were eager to share their wealth and not leave a penny unspent. To finance it, they contributed the equivalent of 300 days in wages—100 from Ménétra alone. But the celebration spoke, too, of their fierce bonds of brotherhood. Ménétra unknowingly foreshadowed the sense of fraternity that would help animate the French Revolution when he toasted his fellow glaziers: "My friends, today we are all comrades together and we are proceeding in unison."

Profligacy was not the only vice of the companions. For many of these young men, the tour was a time for sowing wild oats. Entries in Ménétra's *Journal* indicate that he engaged in around 50 sexual liaisons during a period of less than a decade, not including assorted fleeting encounters with prostitutes. These occasions engendered colorful euphemisms in his writings such as "we sacrificed to cupid." Ménétra wrote of

These figures from the 1742 book *Cries of Paris* were among the many vendors who hawked their wares on the streets. "It is impossible," said one observer, "to describe the sound and the accent of all these multitudinous voices when they are raised in chorus."

"WHO'LL BUY A WINDMILL?"

"BROOMS FOR SALE!"

"COFFEE! COFFEE!"

amorous adventures with widows, wives, servant girls, and even a couple of nuns—"two brides of the baby Jesus," as he called them. Far from being ready to settle down or to take responsibility for his actions, Ménétra took off as soon as a girlfriend started to make any demands on him or, worse, showed him "the bulge in the petticoat."

The young glazier and other companions took special delight in cuckolding their bosses. Ménétra told of a farcical instance of this that took place in Auch, near Toulouse, where he was working on the cathedral's glass paintings. He transmitted syphilis to the boss's wife, who passed it on to her husband, who then consulted his employee, Ménétra, because of his reputation for skill in folk medicine. Ménétra recommended "a little recipe for corns," as he sometimes referred to the disease. The home remedy, which was probably a mercury-based compound, cured all three of them, and Ménétra left town still on good terms with his unsuspecting boss.

Ménétra's *Journal* exhibits a sensibility that strikes the modern reader as twisted and cruel. Not all of his sexual conquests were by the woman's consent, for example; he casually admitted to several rapes. He and his companions frequently took pleasure in tormenting others. In Lyon, when an official summoned all the hunchbacks of the town to a house where they were subjected to ridicule, Ménétra thought it a "delightful farce." In Carpentras, where Jews were strictly segregated in a ghetto, he and several companions stole "two fine chickens" and rationalized the theft on the grounds that their Jewish victim wasn't wearing the yellow hat required by local law as a symbol of his religion. In Bayonne, Ménétra laughed when a group of prostitutes were locked up in an iron cage and repeatedly dunked into the river; he then went about asking "the whores in these parts if they didn't want to be cleaned up."

Such cruel indifference may have been a regular part of life in a world filled with violence and death. From childhood on,

Ménétra and his companions experienced this dark side of life, and the number of his acquaintances who died was as impressive as his toll of seductions. A friend fell into the river and drowned. Ménétra's cousin accidentally killed a kitchen maid while playing around with a pistol. A drinking partner died after gulping down a bottle of poison he mistook for brandy. At an inn, his roommate got up during the middle of the night and tripped over a corpse. Arguments were nearly always resolved by resorting to violence. A disagreement over a personal insult, a woman, or a misguided prank typically flared into fisticuffs and, on occasion, an organized duel for which swords had to be borrowed.

When Jacques-Louis Ménétra returned to Paris for good in the summer of 1764, he tried to recapture the freewheeling mobility and adventurous times of those seven years on the road. Refusing his father's offer to work in his shop, he changed employers and home addresses a half-dozen times in less than two years. He drank, brawled, womanized, and went dancing in the open-air cafés known as *guinguettes*. Pursuing a longtime fascination with fireworks, which were illegal and had blinded and maimed several of his friends, he put on displays while at the same time serving as a member of the local volunteer fire brigade. He was the first glazier in the brigade, which was made up mostly of cobblers, shoemakers, and harnessmakers who were paid a small annual stipend. Occasionally his risk taking did some good: One day he came upon a burning building, dashed in, found a mother and child asleep in the smoke-filled attic, and hauled them down a rope to safety.

In 1765 Ménétra finally settled down. He married and, after paying 1,000 livres for his master's certificate, went into business for himself, setting up shop not far from his father's establishment. He was nearly 27, the average age for a Frenchman to marry. His bride, Marie-Élisabeth Hénin, the daughter of a wool comber from Picardy and technically Ménétra's social inferior,

STREET LIFE

To escape the routine of daily life, Parisians regular-ly flocked to the city's theaters, operas, and concert halls. But for many of the poorer citizens, recreation and relaxation were often found on the streets and in the parks of the capital. At no charge, friends could stroll along the Champs-Élysées, lovers meet in the Bois de Boulogne, and families amble through the Luxembourg Gardens. A particularly popular form of entertainment was dancing. While the wealthy practiced their steps at private balls, the working classes went to dance halls or, as shown below, danced in the streets.

Actors of the Comédie-Française, the royally sanctioned
theater company founded by Louis XIV in 1680,
perform in a comedy, a dramatic form that rivaled
tragedy as the most popular genre of the 1700s.

THE ENCHANTING FRENCH THEATER

Parisians of the 1700s were passionate about theater and flocked to the Comédie-Française, Théâtre Italien, and Opéra-Comique. To playwrights' dismay, however, aristocrats spent much of the time in their private boxes socializing. But the bourgeois crowd standing in the parterre, or "pit," came to watch. Indeed, playwrights wrote with the parterre in mind—and sometimes packed it with friends on opening night, knowing that a play's fate was often determined by the reaction from the pit.

Voltaire thought theater "the most enchanting of all careers" for writers. "It is there that in one day you may obtain glory," he declared. Actors and actresses shared in the glory but paid a steep price for their celebrity. The church condemned the theater as immoral, and excommunicated all who made their life on the stage. Excommunicated actors and actresses could not legitimately marry, have children, or be buried in consecrated ground. Voltaire disapproved of society's hypocritical treatment of stage performers: "We delight to live with them," he observed, "and object to be buried with them; we admit them to our tables, and close our cemeteries to them."

An actress greets patrons in a private box. The private theater boxes of the wealthy were often the venues for lovers' trysts.

Alternative theater also flourished in 18th-century France, with performances staged streetside, at fairgrounds, and in taverns.

The popular performer Mademoiselle Clairon helped revolutionize her craft when she abandoned the traditional singsong delivery of lines.

·Care· 1757 ·

brought 1,000 livres of her own money to the marriage, thus placing the Ménétra couple solidly in the ranks of the petite bourgeoisie. They would have four children, only two of whom—a boy and a girl—survived their periods with wet nurses. Ménétra, unlike his own father, was a devoted parent who supervised his children's education and took them for walks and to concerts. The son would become a glazier; the daughter would marry a pastrymaker and eventually divorce him after a new law made that possible in 1792.

Ménétra was, for a time, a devoted husband as well. A measure of his affection was the profound anxiety he experienced during a public riot in May 1770, five years into the marriage. To celebrate the wedding of the king's grandson—the future Louis XVI—to Marie-Antoinette, the city staged a spectacular fireworks display near the river. The crowd was so large that, afterward, people became trapped in the square known as Place Louis XV and frantically began pushing and shoving. During the resulting riot, which claimed 132 lives, Ménétra and his wife lost sight of each other.

"At the end of the Rue Saint-Honoré," he wrote, "I saw some men carrying a woman dressed like my wife. I hesitated. It turned out not to be her. I went home. Nobody. I was really worried." Ménétra saw his neighbors come home barefoot, "some of the women with their ears torn off. . . . Finally my wife returned home safe and sound and all we could do was wail over that fatal celebration which was like a prelude to the misfortune of the French."

Ménétra's business prospered as Paris grew. His wife, though illiterate, was an efficient and frugal manager. They opened a second shop nearby to make and market "the little manufactured glass objects" he had designed. Soon, however, conflicts over control of the children and of the purse strings disrupted their marriage. "Getting ahead was her main passion," he wrote, "and mine was to enjoy myself. It was impossible to reconcile the two." What he viewed as her miserliness and domineering ways provided a convenient excuse for his philandering. Twice Marie-Élisabeth left him. In his *Journal* he admitted to a dozen extramarital affairs: "I was always looking for ways to keep from getting bored," he later recalled.

He also found diversion by making the acquaintance of prominent and interesting men. Paris was somewhat egalitarian in that men of different rank and fortune rubbed elbows on the streets and in places of public amusement. Ménétra loved the theater, and he often went nightly to the shows on the broad boulevards that stretched from north of the city toward the elegant western sections. He knew leading figures—Gaspard Taconnet, the actor; Jean-Baptiste Nicolet, the producer; Pierre Gourlin, the harlequin clown—and visited them backstage or shared a bottle in a nearby tavern. Ménétra even got to know the public hangman, Henri Samson, who happened to be something of a scholar and folk healer. When Ménétra suffered a kind of paralysis, Samson cured him with a potion brewed from the body of a newly executed criminal. Samson also treated the syphilis of an old girlfriend of Ménétra and her clergyman lover. "His profession aside," Ménétra wrote of the executioner, "he was a gentle, friendly, kindly man."

The most remarkable relationship Ménétra claimed was with the philosophe Jean-Jacques Rousseau. Apparently he met Rousseau in 1770 while working in the writer's old boardinghouse on the Rue Platrière. Rousseau only recently had returned from exile in England after the Parlement of Paris had condemned his writings in 1762. Out of pride he had forsworn the usual practice of such men of letters who lived on gifts from private benefactors and was earning a modest income by copying music for aristocratic clients.

The two men struck up a conversation and began to compare notes. Both were the sons of humble artisans—Rousseau's father was a watchmaker from Geneva—and both had lost their mothers at an early age. Both had rebelled against their fathers

Parisians carouse in the Courtille, a tavern run by Jean Ramponeau. Ramponeau, whose portrait is on the tavern's chimney, served beggars and nobles alike, including an incognito Marie-Antoinette.

and spent years on the road. Both had sired a string of illegitimate children, though Rousseau expressed guilt about his illicit offspring while Ménétra boasted about his.

In his writings Rousseau romanticized working-class artisans like Ménétra. For his part, Ménétra thought the writer an affable and unaffected companion. They became friendly and would go for walks together. "I saw a worried thoughtful man," observed Ménétra. "He stopped to examine every tree and spoke to me very little."

One Sunday they went to the Champs-Élysées to watch tennis, a game then played by up to five players on a side wielding wood-and-parchment rackets called *battoirs*. Afterward they stopped in at the Café de la Régence to drink beer. The two men were dressed alike, although their faces reflected an age difference of 26 years. "We both wore gray suits and round wigs with three rows of curls," recalled Ménétra. "The only difference was that he carried his hat in his hand and my habit was always to wear mine on my head. Both of us had the same clothes but not at all the same [breadth of] knowledge. Between us [the difference] was like night and day."

Inside the café, Rousseau ordered a pitcher of beer, then challenged his younger friend to chess, a game then coming into fashion. Ménétra did not know how to play, so they had a game of checkers instead. Rousseau won. People in the café crowded around to watch the famous writer play, even clambering up on the marble tables for a better view. The following Sunday the proprietor refused Rousseau and Ménétra admission because so many tables had been broken in the commotion.

Ménétra shared Rousseau's antagonism toward much in the old regime. Like Rousseau, the glazier hated the established hierarchy of wealth and privilege and was fiercely anticlerical. During his days on the road he had been exposed to both Judaism and Protestantism, and he questioned the Roman Catholic Church's right to judge either. He considered all religions equally valid—or invalid. He continued to believe in a Supreme Being while rejecting all the theological and ceremonial trappings he had absorbed as an altar boy. "I . . . will never believe that any being on earth is capable of calling a God down to an altar at will," he declared.

Like the Enlightenment iconoclasts, he believed in reason. The Eucharistic host was bread and nothing else. "We even worship a piece of dough which we eat in the firm belief that it is God," Ménétra wrote. "After praying to him and worshiping him in order to satisfy him we've got to eat him too." He would fondly reminisce that in his traveling days he had invented a mock compagnonnage called "companions of the loaf," with its own farcical versions of baptism and the Eucharist. "The whole thing was just to drink and break bread together and laugh and have a good time."

In 1789, just when he had passed age 50 and begun "to lead a quieter life," the freedom and fraternity that Ménétra had always espoused were put to the test. That year he and his neighbors and all of Paris were swept into the maelstrom of the French Revolution. "The word liberty so often repeated had an almost supernatural effect and invigorated us all." He became a citizen-soldier and participated in the overthrow of King Louis XVI in 1792, barely eluding death at the sword of a Swiss Guard. He was a militant in the assembly of his local section, one of the 48 electoral and political units into which Paris was divided in 1790. Slowly, however, his enthusiasm began to ebb. "The French breathed blood," he wrote. "They were like cannibals and were real man-eaters. Neighbor cold-bloodedly denounced neighbor. Blood ties were forgotten. I witnessed those days of horror."

Ménétra, of all people, was accused by his best friend of "moderatism" and summoned before his sectional assembly. Exonerated by the assembly, he survived his own excesses and those of the Terror. "I have seen the Revolution close up," he later reflected. "It was a terrible lesson."

"Liberté!"

A confluence of many events and injustices brought an end to the reign of Louis XVI. The public began to grow more resentful of the arbitrary power of the monarch, who continued to tax the poorer classes heavily while also beginning to increase taxation on the wealthy, including the clergy and nobility, traditionally accorded preferential treatment. The philosophes found France's absolute monarchy and the privileges of class incompatible with their rational approach to the world. But the greatest catalyst of all, perhaps, was the fact that France was close to bankruptcy and the king was out of fund-raising options.

Louis and his advisers decided their only recourse was to press for radical reforms, such as a tax on all landowners, including the nobility. Not surprisingly, the nobles disagreed, and after several confrontations, the king agreed to call the Estates–General, a national assembly that had not met since 1614, to settle the matter.

The commoners eagerly anticipated the convening of the Estates-General. They were by far the majority of the French population but had no political power; they hoped the meeting set for May 5, 1789, would provide an opportunity for true governmental reform. But they soon found out that the achievement of their goals—put into words in 1793 and inscribed in the emblem above: "Unity and indivisibility of the republic. Liberty, equality, fraternity or death"—would require a revolution.

The End of Despotism

The Estates-General was divided into three separate chambers, one each for the clergy, the nobility, and the commoners. This meant that the Third Estate, the commoners, could always be outvoted by the others, who naturally were determined to preserve their privileges. The commoners resolved to take matters into their own hands. On June 17, 1789, the delegates of the Third Estate passed a resolution declaring that they alone constituted the National Assembly of the French People. They thus challenged not only the First and Second Estates, but also the direct authority of the king, who ordered them to disband. Refusing, they reconvened at an indoor tennis court and vowed to remain until they had drafted a new constitution *(right)*.

Although Louis eventually was forced to recognize the new assembly and ordered deputies of the nobility and clergy to join it, he had no intention of distributing his power. He ordered troops to Versailles and Paris, where citizens quickly formed a militia—the National Guard—and began scouring the city for guns and ammunition. On July 14, a crowd looking for gunpowder stormed the Bastille, the prison long despised as a symbol of royal tyranny. At the order of the prison's governor, defenders of the fortress opened fire, killing or wounding about 200 people. A group of army mutineers armed with cannon soon joined the militia, however, and the prison's commandant surrendered.

When told the news, King Louis XVI is said to have asked, "Is it a revolt?" "No, sire," his aide replied, "It's a revolution."

After taking the Bastille and releasing its few prisoners, the crowd seizes its governor. His severed head was later raised in triumph on a pike.

On August 26, 1789, the assembly passed the Declaration of the Rights of Man and of the Citizen, which became the basis for a new constitution.

Fall of the Monarchy

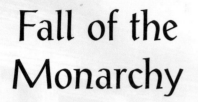

On October 5, 1789, the women of Paris were fuming: The king had rejected the assembly's reforms and, despite a good harvest, bread was still in short supply. There is no evidence that Marie-Antoinette, when told of the shortage, had callously remarked, "Let them eat cake," but the story shows the public's distrust of the royals. A crowd of angry women gathered, chanting, "When will we have bread?" The throng—some 6,000 strong—marched to Versailles. Joined by the National Guard, they demanded bread and the king's return to Paris. The king agreed to their demands, but the mob killed two royal guards and thrust their heads on pikes, holding them aloft as they escorted the royal family—and wagons full of flour—back to Paris (above).

The royal family settled into a wary existence at the Tuileries, and the assembly set to work on a constitution, adopted in 1791, transforming France into a constitutional monarchy. But further conflicts ensued, and an armed mob attacked the palace on August 10, 1792. The assembly voted to suspend the monarchy and sent Louis and his family to the Temple prison.

The new Constitutional Convention elected later that month abolished the monarchy and declared France a republic. The following January, Louis XVI, now called Louis the Last, was convicted of conspiring against national liberty. He was sent to the guillotine on January 21, 1793; his queen followed in October.

Parisians and National Guardsmen attack the Tuileries in 1792. The king escaped, but some 800 of his men and 400 insurgents were killed (right).

An executioner displays the head of Louis XVI. The guillotine had been adopted early in the revolution as a humane form of death.

A Time of Turmoil

Since April 1792, France had been at war with Austria, whose ruler was thought to be fomenting counterrevolution. In February 1793, France declared war against England, Holland, and Spain. The convention conscripted 300,000 men to fight, but many experienced officers had left the army earlier in the revolution, the new troops were poorly trained, and the commanding general, frustrated by interference from Paris, deserted to the Austrians in April 1793. In short, the French army was in disarray.

The revolutionary government also had to fight an enemy within its own borders. Economic conditions had worsened in parts of the country, including the Vendée, in western France. Citizens there were opposed to many of the revolution's goals, and they were unwilling to fight for a cause they did not support. In March 1793 they began attacks against the National Guard and French troops.

But while the revolution suffered setbacks in some parts of the country, in Paris and most other areas its backers held firm, spurred on by radical journalists such as Jean-Paul Marat and the working poor known as sans-culottes *(far right)*. The sans-culottes—so called because they wore long pants rather than the knee breeches, or culottes, of the upper classes—began to take justice into their own hands, and gradually came under the control of extremists.

Singing troops march across a song sheet of the *Marseillaise,* the stirring revolutionary anthem credited with raising 100,000 men for the army.

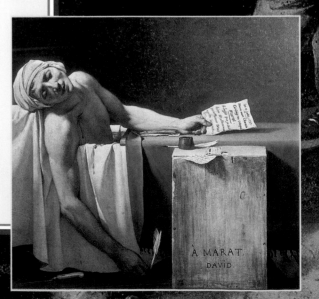

Revolutionary journalist Jean-Paul Marat, who was stabbed in his bath in July 1793, had called for death for his political opponents.

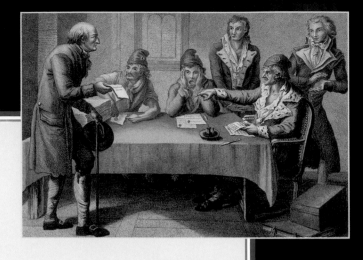

The Reign of Terror

In response to the turmoil of war and resistance to the revolution, laws to strengthen the government were passed and committees were established to restore order. One such group—the Committee of Public Safety, which oversaw the war effort—was dominated by Maximilien Robespierre. A lawyer and member of the National Assembly in 1789, Robespierre had been a leader in the revolution.

The convention also established the Revolutionary Tribunal to prosecute suspected counterrevolutionaries. Between April 1793 and May 1794, the Paris tribunal convicted and executed some 2,750 people. Zealous provincial tribunals executed another 40,000 people during the winter of 1793-1794.

Before spring arrived, Robespierre turned on former supporters, arresting the leaders of the sans-culottes, who had complained about high prices and low wages. Next was minister of justice Georges-Jacques Danton and his followers. It was because Danton and his men "tried to halt the action of the guillotine that they will have to suffer it themselves," wrote one observer. In June of that year, amid the frenzy of what was known as the Great Terror, Robespierre called for yet another round of retribution, which took the lives of almost 1,400 men and women in Paris over a span of six weeks. The painting at far right depicts prisoners waiting for their turn at the guillotine. As one radical was led away, she cried, "O Liberty, what crimes are committed in your name."

Damned by pointing fingers, a defendant appears before a tribunal. By June 1794 laws protecting the accused were so weak they did not allow for defense witnesses or even a lawyer.

During the height of the terror, Robespierre proposed a new civic religion and organized the Festival of the Supreme Being (below), "whose true priest . . . is nature."

The Revolution Is Over

The Great Terror claimed some 200 people a week under blatantly unjust and vaguely worded laws. By midsummer, convention members turned against Robespierre, and on July 27, they publicly denounced him. "Silence, murderer!" one commanded. "Danton's blood is running from your mouth, it's choking you!" Confusion followed: Robespierre was arrested, a rescue effort failed, and he shot himself, shattering his jaw. The next day a bandaged Robespierre was executed with 80 of his supporters *(far right)*. A driving force of the revolution was dead, but the terror was over.

A period of drift followed. Groups of *jeunesse dorée,* or gilded youth *(below, left),* roamed the streets, fighting with sans-culottes, destroying busts of Marat, and denouncing Robespierre. In August 1795 a new constitution established the Directory, a five-man council with executive power over a legislative body. But in a move reminiscent of the days of *l'ancien régime,* only the propertied classes could vote. The Directory ruled for four years, until military hero Napoleon Bonaparte returned from the front and overthrew them on November 9, 1799. He declared the revolution over and embarked on an autocratic regime to rival that of a French king.

With what Napoleon called "a whiff of grapeshot," his troops put down the last outbreak of violence of the French revolution.

Rightfully wary of Napoleon's ambition and popularity, the convention banished him to fight in Italy in 1796.

GLOSSARY

Absolute monarchy: a state ruled by a hereditary monarch who holds ultimate personal authority and discretionary power.

Académie Française: the literary academy, established in 1635 by Cardinal Richelieu, charged with upholding literary standards and maintaining the purity of the French language.

Academy of Sciences: the official state institution for scientific research, founded in 1666.

Adieu: goodbye; farewell.

Ancien régime: literally, "old regime." The political and social system that existed in France prior to the revolution of 1789.

Anglophile: one who admires England, its people, customs, institutions, and culture.

Baquet: a tub, with or without a lid, such as the large, lidded tub Mesmer used to "magnetize" up to 30 people simultaneously.

Bastille: in Paris, the medieval fortress used in the 17th and 18th centuries as a prison, which became a symbol of royal despotism. Stormed by Parisians on July 14, 1789, it was later demolished by the revolutionary government.

Battoir: the wood-and-parchment racket used in the 18th-century form of tennis.

Bloodletting: also known as "breathing a vein." The therapeutic removal of blood from a patient by opening a vein.

Boudoir: a woman's dressing room, bedroom, or private sitting room.

Bourgeois: originally, anyone who lived within a walled town or city. Later, any person belonging to the middle class.

Bourgeoisie: the middle class; those socially lower than the nobility but higher than the laboring class.

Calvinist: one who adheres to the tenets of John Calvin. Calvinism is a religion that stresses the omnipotence of God, the doctrine of predestination, and the salvation of the elect through God's grace alone.

Ce pays-ci: literally, "this country." Name by which French nobles referred to themselves, their society, and their surroundings.

Château: in France, a castle, feudal fortress, mansion, palace, large country manor, or estate.

Chevalier: in prerevolutionary France, a nobleman of the lowest rank.

Comédie-Française: the influential national theater company of France, founded in 1680.

Compagnon: a journeyman who has completed his apprenticeship but who, before being admitted to a guild as a master, must work under other masters for six or more years.

Compagnonnage: any of the three French labor associations for compagnons (journeymen).

Comte: a count; a European nobleman ranking below a marquis.

Comtesse: a countess; wife or widow of a comte.

Constitutional monarchy: a monarchy in which the powers of the ruler are limited to those granted by a constitution.

Corvée: a tax paid in labor; unpaid labor owed by a peasant to a lord or to the monarch.

Coucher: to go or be put to bed. In the case of the French king, the last public ritual in his day.

Court of Peers: the high nobility of France.

Dauphin: the eldest son of the king of France; used as a title from 1349 through 1830.

Dévots: a conservative ultrareligious faction in 18th-century France.

Directory: the five-man executive branch of the republican government of France, established by the French constitution of 1795, and which proved to be weak and corrupt.

Divine right of kings: the doctrine that a king is sacred, that his power and authority are God-given, and that he cannot be held accountable for his actions by any earthly authority.

Duc: a duke; a nobleman of the highest hereditary rank after that of a prince.

Duchesse: the wife or widow of a duke; a woman who holds the title to a duchy in her own right.

Duchy: the territory of a duke or duchess.

Edict of Nantes: a 1593 decree granting partial religious freedom to the Huguenots, thus ending 46 years of religious wars in France. Revoked in 1685 by Louis XIV, depriving French Protestants of all religious and civil liberties.

Encyclopédistes: Enlightenment philosophes who contributed to the *Encyclopédie*.

Enlightenment: a philosophical movement marked by a rejection of traditional social, religious, and political ideas and a belief in the power of reason.

Estates-General: in prerevolutionary France, the representative assembly of the three estates: clergy, nobility, and commoners.

First Estate: in prerevolutionary France, one of the three estates into which the population was divided; the First Estate was the clergy.

Freemasons: a fraternal organization that spread internationally in the 1700s, providing a vehicle for the transmission of practices of freedom of association and the philosophical and political ideas and ideals of the Enlightenment.

Fronde: a series of civil wars in France between 1648 and 1653 sparked by opposition to the policies of Cardinal Mazarin.

Gavotte: a dance of French peasant origin resembling the minuet.

Grenadier: from the late 16th century through World War I, foot soldiers specially trained to throw grenades, generally organized into separate, elite companies within battalions.

Guillotine: a device for beheading a person consisting of a heavy, sharp blade that falls freely between two grooved upright posts surmounted by a crossbeam for stability.

Guinguette: an open-air café or small tavern, usually with a pleasure garden.

Haute bourgeoisie: the upper middle class; financiers and other professionals, with wealth equal to or surpassing that of the nobility and with whom the nobility often intermarried.

Huguenots: French Protestants, persecuted by both the Catholics and the French government for their beliefs and their republican internal organizational structure.

Intendants: royal administrators who served as agents of the king in the 30 French provinces from about 1640 to 1789, usurping the power of local officials and nobles.

Jeunesse dorée: literally, "gilded youth." Fashionably dressed right-wing gangs formed after the collapse of the Reign of Terror that denounced Robespierre and Jacobins in general and assaulted the sans-culottes in the streets.

Journeyman: originally, one hired for a day's work. Later, a worker who has served his apprenticeship in a craft or trade and is qualified to work for someone else but who has not yet qualified as a master.

La Marseillaise: the French national anthem, composed in 1792 as a marching song for troops heading into battle against Austria and brought to Paris by revolutionary activists from the city of Marseilles. It was accepted by the convention as the national anthem in 1795.

Lansquenet: a card game popular in 18th-century France.

Lettre de cachet: a letter under the seal of the king, commanding the recipient to obey the orders issued therein and often ordering the immediate imprisonment of the recipient, without trial, for an indefinite period of time.

Lever: literally, "to rise." The first royal ritual of the day in which the king arose from his bed in the State Bedchamber and received the highest-ranking French nobles.

Leyden jar: a jar for storing an electric charge.

Libertine: one who acts without moral or sexual restraint; a freethinker in religious matters who defies established religious dogma.

Lieutenant general of police: the chief of police, who had enormous power in Paris and was responsible for the security, quality of life, and welfare of its inhabitants.

Lieux à l'angloise: literally, "English place." Name given to the English flush toilet.

L'infâme: Voltaire's term for the religious superstition and intolerance fomented and engaged in by the Catholic Church and its supporters.

Livre: a former French monetary unit originally worth one pound of silver.

L'opinion publique: literally, "public opinion." Beginning with discussions in the salons, coffeehouses, and academies of Paris, it spread through books, pamphlets, and newspapers and it was recognized as a relatively new force in French society by the mid-18th century.

Louvre: an 18th-century royal palace in Paris, now the national museum and art gallery.

Madame: a French title of respect used before a married woman's surname, equivalent to Mrs.

Marquis: a European nobleman ranking below a duke but above a count.

Marquise: the wife or widow of a marquis; a woman who is a marquise in her own right.

Meter: the unit of length, now used internationally, chosen by the French Academy of Sciences in 1791 to replace the traditional weights and measures of the old regime.

Mofette: literally, "noxious fume"; Lavoisier's term for air that he deemed unfit to breathe.

Monseigneur: a French title of honor and respect for princes and prelates.

Monsieur: a French title of respect and a form of address, used either alone or before a man's name or title and generally equivalent to Mr. or sir.

Mouches: literally, "flies"; Parisians' name for the police force's informers.

National Guard: the citizens' militia of Paris begun at the start of the French Revolution.

Nouveau riche: literally, "new rich." One who has recently become rich, especially one who flaunts the new wealth or is uncultured.

Ombre: a card game, similar to whist, for three players using, in France, 52 cards; popular in the 17th and 18th centuries throughout Europe.

Opéra-Comique: a French form of opera differing from classical opera in that spoken dialogue is interspersed with self-contained musical numbers throughout the work.

Palais: the palace or official residence of a reigning monarch and sometimes the seat of government.

Pandoras: wooden dolls that were dressed in the most recent court fashions and sent to Paris and other cities to be copied.

Pannier: a hoop skirt. A woman's undergarment having a flat front and rear but extending as much as nine feet on each side of the wearer.

Panthéon: the national mausoleum in Paris, built as a church but transformed during the revolution into a temple to house the remains and perpetuate the memory of the dead.

Parlements: under *l'ancien régime*, the 13 royal courts of law that both administered the law and served as supreme courts of appeal. The parlements registered the king's edicts prior to their becoming law but had no independent power to levy taxes or enact legislation.

Parterre: the part of the main floor of a theater directly behind the orchestra.

Petite bourgeoisie: the lower middle class, including small shopkeepers, tradesmen, and craftsmen with modest incomes.

Petits Appartements: at Versailles, a private suite in which only the king's most intimate friends and family were welcome.

Philosophes: literally, "philosophers." Generally, the philosophical, political, scientific, or social thinkers and writers associated with the 18th-century French Enlightenment; they supported social, economic, cultural, and political reforms.

Phlogiston: a substance that, prior to the discovery of oxygen, was thought to be a volatile part of combustible material, released in burning and thought to be involved in respiration.

Population flottante: the hundreds of thousands of peasants who could not make a living from the land and drifted throughout France scavenging food and stealing to survive.

Prelate: a high-ranking member of the clergy.

Prince of the blood: a prince who was a direct descendant of an earlier French king.

Protégé: someone whose welfare, education, and/or career is promoted or furthered by a person of influence, wealth, or experience.

Protégée: a female protégé.

Question: the torture accompanying the legal interrogation process under *l'ancien régime*. In the two degrees of torture, ordinary and extraordinary, a person's arms and legs could be stretched and pulled from their sockets or the victim might be force fed gallons of water, ballooning the body to twice its normal size.

Regent: one who rules during the minority, absence, or incapacitation of a monarch.

Reign of Terror: the period of the French Revolution during which the Committee of Public Safety was in control of the government and suspected enemies of the revolution were arrested and often executed; its final months are known as the Great Terror.

Republic of letters: the intellectual community that arose during the 17th and 18th centuries.

Revolutionary Tribunal: the court set up by the National Convention to prosecute enemies of the revolution, particularly nobles, priests, and other suspected counterrevolutionaries.

Royal brevet: an order by a monarch, directing a person or group to take some action or perform some task.

Royal pension: part of a system of royal patronage under which the king granted an annual state pension.

Salon: a large, elegant room for receiving and entertaining guests. A periodic gathering of guests of social, intellectual, artistic, literary, or political prominence for discussion.

Salonnière: a woman who presides, in her salon, over a regular social gathering for the purpose of discussion.

Sans-culotte: during the French Revolution, radical republican activists, generally from the class of workers and artisans, so called because they wore the long trousers of the laboring class rather than the knee breeches of the rich and noble.

Second Estate: in prerevolutionary France, one of the three estates, or social orders, into which the population was divided; the Second Estate was the nobility.

Siècle des lumières: literally, "century of lights." The term for the Enlightenment, used by the philosophes to describe their century.

Swiss Guard: a member of a corps of elite soldiers of Swiss birth used in prerevolutionary France to guard the king.

Théâtre des Petits Cabinets: the tiny theater of Madame de Pompadour, who recruited courtiers as actors and musicians.

Third Estate: in prerevolutionary France, one of the three estates, or social orders, into which the population was divided; the Third Estate consisted of everyone who was not part of either the nobility or the clergy.

Versailles: the site, southwest of Paris, of a magnificent French palace, gardens, and parkland, built in the mid-1600s for Louis XIV.

Water closet: a toilet, often enclosed in a small booth.

PRONUNCIATION GUIDE

Académie ah-kah-day-MEE
Adelaïde ah-deh-lah-EED
Alembert AH-LAHN-BEHR
Ancien régime AHN-SYAHN ray-ZHEEM
Baquet bah-KAY
Bastille bah-STEEL
Blanchard BLAHN-SHAHR
Boucher boo-SHAY
Boudoir BOO-dwahr
Bourbon BOOR-bohn
Bourgeois boor-ZHWAH
Bourgeoisie boor-zhwah-ZEE
Brissot BREE-SOH
Calas CAH-LAH
Ce pays-ci suh pay-ee-SEE
Chantilly shahn-tee-YEE
Chartres SHAHR-treh
Châteauroux SHAH-toh-roo
Château shah-TOH
Châtelet shah-tuh-LAY
Châtillon shah-tee-OHN
Chat sauvage SHAH soh-VAHZH
Chevalier SHEH-vahl-yay
Choisy shwah-ZEE
Chroniques scandaleuses kroh-NEEK SKAHN-dah-lyeuhz
Comédie-Française koh-may-DEE-frahn-SEHZ
Compagnon kohm-pahn-YOHN
Condorcet COHN-dohr-SAY
Dauphin doh-FAN
Deffand deh-FAHN
Destouches day-TOOSH
Dictionnaire philosophique dee-syoh-NEHR fee-loh-zoh-FEEK

Diderot DEE-droh
Fontainebleau fohn-tehn-BLOH
Fronde frohnd
Galerie des Glaces gahl-REE day GLAHS
Geoffrin zhoh-FRAN
Guibert gee-BEHR
Huguenot yoo-GNOH
Jeunesse dorée zhuh-NESS doh-RAY
Laclos lah-CLOH
Lagrange lah-GRAHNZH
La Henriade lah EHN-ree-AHD
Lansquenet LAHN-keh-nay
La Place lah plahs
La Raincy lah REHN-see
Lavoisier lah-VWAHZ-yay
Lespinasse LEHS-pee-nahs
L'état, c'est moi lay-TAH, SAY MWAH
Lettre de cachet LEH-treh duh kah-SHAY
Lever leh-VAY
Lieux à l'angloise lih-YUH ah lahn-GLWAHZ
Louis lwee
Louvre LOOV-reh
Lumière loo-MYEHR
Mailly-Nesle may-YEE-nehl
Marmontel mahr-mohn-TEHL
Marseillaise mahr-seh-YEHZ
Mofette MOHF-eht
Molière moh-LYEHR
Monsieur muh-SYEUH
Montesquieu MOHN-teh-SKYEUH
Montgolfier MOHN-GAWL-FYAY
Necker NEH-KEHR
Opéra-Comique OH-PEH-RAH-koh-MEEK

Orléans ohr-lay-AHN
Palais-Royal pal-AY-rwah-YAHL
Panthéon PAN-tay-OHN
Parlement PAHR-luh-mahn
Paulze pawlz
Philippe FEE-LEEP
Philosophe FEE-loh-zohf
Poisson pwah-SOHN
Pompadour POHN-pah-door
Prie pree
Racine rah-SEEN
Richelieu REE-shyuhl-yuh
Robespierre ROH-behs-pyehr
Rousseau roo-SOH
Rue Saint-Dominique ROO SAN-DOH-mee-NEEK
Saint-Denis SAN-duh-NEE
Salonnière sah-LAHN-yehr
Sans-culottes SAHN-kyoo-LAHT
Seine sehnn
Sèvres SEHV-reh
Siècle des lumières see-EK-leh day loo-MYEHR
Soirée swah-RAY
Théâtre des Petits Cabinets tay-AH-treh day puh-TEE kah-bee-NAY
Toilette twah-LET
Toulouse too-LOOZ
Tout va bien TOO VAH bih-YEHN
Turgot TUHR-GOH
Ventadour VEHN-tah-door
Versailles vehr-SEYE
Vigée-Lebrun VEE-ZHAY-luh-BRUHN
Vincennes van-SEHNN
Voltaire vohl-TEHR

ACKNOWLEDGMENTS AND PICTURE CREDITS

ACKNOWLEDGMENTS

The editors wish to thank the following individuals and institutions for their valuable assistance in the preparation of this volume:

Séverine Burgelin, RMN, Paris; Arthur Hermann, Washington, D.C.; Heidrun Klein, Bildarchiv Preussischer Kulturbesitz, Berlin; Marie Montembault, Département des Antiquités Grecques et Romaines, Musée du Louvre, Paris.

Orti, Paris. **119:** Photo Bulloz, Paris; National Gallery of Scotland, Edinburgh (detail of *Boy with a Lesson Book* by J.-B. Greuze). **120:** Photo Josse, Paris. **122-124:** Jean-Loup Charmet, Paris. **126, 127:** Lauros-Giraudon, Paris. **129:** Jean-Loup Charmet, Paris. **131:** © Christie's Images, Ltd. 1999. **132:** Gianni Dagli Orti, Paris; Giraudon, Paris. **133:** Musée Carnavalet/Bulloz/Bridgeman Art Library, London. **134:** Jean-Loup Charmet, Paris. **136, 137:** Border by John Drummond, © Time Life Inc.; Lauros-Giraudon, Paris; Louvre/AKG, Paris. **138, 139:** From *The Eighteenth Century, Its Institutions, Customs, and Costumes,* by Paul Lacroix, Scribner, Welford, and Armstrong, New York, 1876. **141:** Gianni Dagli Orti, Paris. **142, 143:** Border by John Drummond, © Time Life Inc.; Photo Bulloz, Paris; from *Le Theatre a Paris Au XVIIIe Siècle,* Librairie de France, 1927; from *Die Sitten Des Rokoko,* Herausgegeben von Franz Blei, Georg Müller Verlag, Munich, 1921—Jean-Loup Charmet, Paris. **144:** Gianni Dagli Orti, Paris. **145:** Photo Bulloz, Paris. **147-151:** Tallandier (tricolor ribbon). **147:** Background Château de Versailles/Bulloz/Bridgeman Art Library, London—Jean-Loup Charmet, Paris. **148, 149:** Musée Carnavalet/Bulloz/Bridge-man Art Library, London; Château de Versailles/Bulloz/Bridgeman Art Library, London—Musée Carnavalet/Giraudon/Bridgeman Art Library, London. **150, 151:** Photo Bulloz, Paris (3)—Selva, Paris. **152, 153:** Lauros-Giraudon, Paris; Photo Bulloz, Paris—Artothek, Peissenberg/Musée d'Art Ancien, Brussels. **154, 155:** Photo Bulloz, Paris; Selva, Paris—Lauros-Giraudon, Paris. **156, 157:** Giraudon, Paris; Photo Bulloz, Paris; Jean Vigne—Photo Josse, Paris.

Design elements: John Drummond, © Time Life Inc.

BIBLIOGRAPHY

BOOKS

Adhémar, Jean. *Graphic Art of the 18th Century.* Trans. by M. I. Martin. New York: McGraw-Hill, 1964.

Ardagh, John. *Cultural Atlas of France.* New York: Facts On File, 1991.

Bajou, Thierry. *Paintings at Versailles: XVIIth Century.* Trans. by Elizabeth Wiles-Portier. Paris: Buchet/Chastel, 1998.

Baker, Keith Michael:
Condorcet: From Natural Philosophy to Social Mathematics. Chicago: University of Chicago Press, 1975.
Inventing the French Revolution. Cambridge: Cambridge University Press, 1990.

Bernier, Olivier:
The Eighteenth-Century Woman. Garden City, N.Y.: Doubleday, 1981.
Louis the Beloved: The Life of Louis XV. Garden City, N.Y.: Doubleday, 1984.

Blondel, Jacques-François. *De la Distribution des Maisons de Plaisance, et de la Decoration des Edifices en General.* Farnborough, Hants, England: Gregg Press, 1967 (reprint of 1738 edition).

Blum, Carol. *Diderot: The Virtue of a Philosopher.* New York: Viking Press, 1974.

Bouissounouse, Janine. *Julie: The Life of Mademoiselle de Lespinasse.* Trans. by Pierre de Fontnouvelle. New York: Appleton-Century-Crofts, 1962.

Braudel, Fernand. *The Structures of Everyday Life: The Limits of the Possible.* Vol. 1 of *Civilization and Capitalism: 15th-18th Century.* New York: Harper & Row, 1979.

Buranelli, Vincent. *The Wizard from Vienna.* London: Peter Owen, 1975.

Burke, Peter. *The Fabrication of Louis XIV.* New Haven, Conn.: Yale University Press, 1992.

Chastel, André. *French Art: The Ancien Régime, 1620-1775.* Trans. by Deke Dusinberre. Paris: Flammarion, 1995.

Cobb, Richard, ed. *Voices of the French Revolution.* Topsfield, Mass.: Salem House, 1988.

Cobban, Alfred, et al. *The Eighteenth Century: Europe in the Age of Enlightenment.* Ed. by Alfred Cobban. New York: McGraw-Hill, 1969.

Cohen, I. Bernard. *Album of Science: From Leonardo to Lavoisier, 1450-1800.* New York: Charles Scribner's Sons, 1980.

Conisbee, Philip. *Painting in Eighteenth-Century France.* Ithaca, N.Y.: Cornell University Press, 1981.

Constans, Claire. *Versailles: Absolutism and Harmony.* New York: Vendome Press, 1998.

Craveri, Benedetta. *Madame du Deffand and Her World.* Trans. by Teresa Waugh. Boston: David R. Godine, 1982.

Crocker, Lester G., ed. *Diderot's Selected Writings.* Trans. by Derek Coltman. New York: Macmillan, 1966.

Crow, Thomas E. *Painters and Public Life in Eighteenth-Century Paris.* New Haven, Conn.: Yale University Press, 1985.

Dakin, Douglas. *Turgot and the Ancien Régime in France.* New York: Octagon Books, 1965.

Darnton, Robert:
The Forbidden Best-Sellers of Pre-Revolutionary France. New York: W. W. Norton, 1996.
The Great Cat Massacre and Other Episodes in French Cultural History. New York: Vintage Books, 1984.

DeLorme, Eleanor P. *Garden Pavilions and the 18th Century French Court.* Woodbridge, Suffolk, England: Antique Collectors' Club, 1996.

Diderot, Denis:
Diderot Encyclopedia: The Complete Illustrations, 1762-1777, Vol. 2. New York: Harry N. Abrams, 1978.

A Diderot Pictorial Encyclopedia of Trades and Industry, Vol. 2. New York: Dover, 1959.

The Encyclopedia. Ed. and trans. by Stephen J. Gendzier. New York: Harper Torchbooks, 1967.

Donovan, Arthur. *Antoine Lavoisier: Science, Administration, and Revolution.* Oxford: Blackwell, 1993.

Ducros, Louis. *French Society in the Eighteenth Century.* Trans. by W. de Geijer. New York: Burt Franklin, 1971.

Durant, Will, and Ariel Durant:
The Age of Voltaire, Vol. 9 of *The Story of Civilization.* New York: Simon and Schuster, 1965.
Rousseau and Revolution, Vol. 10 of *The Story of Civilization.* New York: MJF Books, 1967.

Eighteenth-Century Women and the Arts. Ed. by Frederick M. Keener and Susan E. Lorsch. New York: Greenwood Press, 1988.

Encyclopedia of the Enlightenment. New York: Facts On File, 1996.

Enlightenment Portraits. Ed. by Michel Vovelle. Chicago: University of Chicago Press, 1997.

Farge, Arlette, and Jacques Revel. *The Vanishing Children of Paris: Rumor and Politics before the French Revolution.* Trans. by Claudia Miéville. Cambridge, Mass.: Harvard University Press, 1991.

Farr, Evelyn. *Before the Deluge: Parisian Society in the Reign of Louis XVI.* London: Peter Owen, 1994.

Florisoone, Michel. *Le Dix-Huitiéme Siécle.* Paris: Editions Pierre Tisné, 1948.

The French Revolution. New York: American Heritage, 1965.

French Women and the Age of Enlightenment. Ed. by Samia I. Spencer. Bloomington: Indiana University Press, 1984.

Garraty, John Arthur. *The Columbia History of the World.* New York: Harper & Row, 1972.

Gay, Peter. *Voltaire's Politics: The Poet as Realist.* New Haven, Conn.: Yale University Press, 1988.

Gay, Peter, and the Editors of Time-Life Books. *Age of Enlightenment* (Great Ages of Man series). New York: Time-Life Books, 1966.

Gelbart, Nina Rattner. *The King's Midwife: A History and Mystery of Madame du Coudray.* Berkeley: University of California Press, 1998.

Gillispie, Charles Coulston:
The Montgolfier Brothers and the Invention of Aviation: 1783-1784. Princeton, N.J.: Princeton University Press, 1983.
Science and Polity in France at the End of the Old Regime. Princeton, N.J.: Princeton University Press, 1980.

Giscard d'Estaing, Valérie-Anne. *The World Almanac of Inventions.* New York: World Almanac, 1985.

Goodman, Dena. *The Republic of Letters: A Cultural History of the French Enlightenment.* Ithaca, N.Y.: Cornell University Press, 1994.

Goubert, Pierre:
The Course of French History. Trans. by Maarten Ultee. New York: Franklin Watts, 1988.
Louis XIV and Twenty Million Frenchmen. Trans. by Anne Carter. New York: Random House, 1970.

Grunfeld, Frederic V. *The French Kings.* Chicago: Stonehenge, 1982.

Guedj, Denis. *La Révolution des Savants.* [Paris]: Découvertes Gallimard Sciences, 1988.

Hammond, Inc. *Historical Atlas of the World.* Maplewood, N.J.: Hammond, 1984.

Hankins, Thomas L.:
Jean d'Alembert: Science and the Enlightenment. Oxford: Clarendon Press, 1970.
Science and the Enlightenment. Cambridge: Cambridge University Press, 1985.

A History of Private Life:
Passions of the Renaissance, Vol. 3. Cambridge, Mass.: Belknap Press, 1989.
From the Fires of Revolution to the Great War, Vol. 4. Trans. by Arthur Goldhammer. Cambridge, Mass.: Belknap Press, 1990.

The How It Works Encyclopedia of Great Inventors & Discoveries. London: Marshall Cavendish Books, 1978.

Hufton, Olwen H. *The Poor of Eighteenth-Century France, 1750-1789.* Oxford: Clarendon Press, 1974.

Jacob, Margaret C. *Living the Enlightenment.* New York: Oxford University Press, 1991.

James, W., and A. Molé. *Dictionary of the French and English Languages.* New York: Macmillan, 1930.

Jones, Colin. *The Cambridge Illustrated History of France.* Cambridge: Cambridge University Press, 1994.

Lacroix, Paul. *France in the Eighteenth Century: Its Institutions, Customs and Costumes.* New York: Frederick Ungar, 1963.

Lucie-Smith, Edward. *Furniture: A Concise History.* New York: Oxford University Press, 1979.

Manceron, Claude. *The French Revolution:*
Twilight of the Old Order, 1774-1778, Vol. 1. Trans. by Patricia Wolf. New York: Alfred A. Knopf, 1977.
The Wind from America, 1778-1781, Vol. 2. Trans. by Nancy Amphoux. New York: Alfred A. Knopf, 1978.
Their Gracious Pleasure, 1782-1785, Vol. 3. Trans. by Nancy Amphoux. New York: Alfred A. Knopf, 1980.
Toward the Brink, 1785-1787, Vol. 4. Trans. by Nancy Amphoux. New York: Alfred A. Knopf, 1983.

Man, Myth & Magic: The Illustrated Encyclopedia of Mythology, Religion and the Unknown. New York: Marshall Cavendish, 1985.

Maza, Sarah C. *Private Lives and Public Affairs.* Berkeley: University of California Press, 1993.

Ménétra, Jacques-Louis. *Journal of My Life.* New York: Columbia University Press, 1986.

Mitford, Nancy:
Madame de Pompadour. New York: Harper & Row, 1968.
The Sun King. London: Penguin Books, 1966.

National Geographic Atlas of the World. Washington, D.C.: National Geographic Society, 1970.

Pevitt, Christine. *Philippe, duc d'Orléans: Regent of France.* New York: Atlantic Monthly Press, 1997.

Poirier, Jean-Pierre. *Lavoisier: Chemist, Biologist, Economist*. Trans. by Rebecca Balinski. Philadelphia: University of Pennsylvania Press, 1996.

Powers of the Crown: TimeFrame AD 1600-1700 (Time Frame series). Alexandria, Va.: Time-Life Books, 1989.

Pratt, N. S. *The French Revolution*. New York: John Day, 1970.

Praz, Mario. *An Illustrated History of Interior Decoration*. London: Thames and Hudson, 1964.

Rand, Richard. *Intimate Encounters*. Princeton, N.J.: Princeton University, 1997.

Reader's Digest. *Everyday Life through the Ages*. London: Reader's Digest, 1992.

Roche, Daniel:
The Culture of Clothing: Dress and Fashion in the 'Ancien Régime.' Trans. by Jean Birrell. Cambridge: Cambridge University Press, 1994.

The People of Paris: An Essay in Popular Culture in the 18th Century. Trans. by Marie Evans. Berkeley: University of California Press, 1981.

Roots of Western Civilization:
Centers of Invention. Danbury, Conn.: Grolier Educational, 1993.
Seats of Power. Danbury, Conn.: Grolier Educational, 1994.

Schama, Simon. *Citizens: A Chronicle of the French Revolution*. New York: Alfred A. Knopf, 1989.

Scott, Katie. *The Rococo Interior*. New Haven, Conn.: Yale University Press, 1995.

Sheriff, Mary D. *The Exceptional Woman: Elisabeth Vigée-Lebrun and the Cultural Politics of Art*. Chicago: University of Chicago Press, 1996.

Thornton, Peter. *Authentic Decor: The Domestic Interior, 1620-1920*. New York: Viking, 1984.

Van Kley, Dale K. *The Damiens Affair*. Princeton, N.J.: Princeton University Press, 1984.

Verlet, Pierre. *The Eighteenth Century in France*. Trans. by George Savage. Rutland, Vt.: Charles E. Tuttle, 1967.

Versailles au Siecle de Louis XIV. Paris: Textuel, 1993.

Voltaire. *Selections*. Ed. by Paul Edwards. New York: Scribner/Macmillan, 1989.

Williams, Alan. *The Police of Paris, 1718-1789*. Baton Rouge: Louisiana State University Press, 1979.

Winds of Revolution: TimeFrame AD 1700-1800 (TimeFrame series). Alexandria, Va.: Time-Life Books, 1990.

PERIODICALS
Les Collections de l'Histoire, June 1998.

OTHER SOURCES
France in the Eighteenth Century. Exhibition. London: Royal Academy of Arts, Winter 1968.

INDEX

Numerals in italics indicate an illustration of the subject mentioned.

Time-Life Books is a division of Time Life Inc.

TIME LIFE INC.
PRESIDENT and CEO: George Artandi

TIME-LIFE BOOKS
PUBLISHER/MANAGING EDITOR: Neil Kagan
SENIOR VICE PRESIDENT, MARKETING:
Joseph A. Kuna
VICE PRESIDENT, NEW PRODUCT
DEVELOPMENT: Amy Golden

What Life Was Like
DURING THE AGE OF REASON

EDITOR: Denise Dersin
DIRECTOR, NEW PRODUCT DEVELOPMENT:
Elizabeth D. Ward
DIRECTOR OF MARKETING: Pamela R. Farrell

Deputy Editor: Paula York-Soderlund
Design Directors: Cynthia T. Richardson,
Barbara M. Sheppard
Text Editor: Robin Currie
Associate Editor/Research and Writing: Trudy W. Pearson
Assistant Art Director: Janet Dell Russell Johnson
Senior Copyeditor: Mary Beth Oelkers-Keegan
Technical Art Specialist: John Drummond
Picture Coordinator: David Herod
Editorial Assistant: Christine Higgins

Special Contributors: Ronald H. Bailey, Ellen Galford,
Dónal Kevin Gordon (chapter text); Gaye Brown, Sarah
L. Evans, Christina Huth, Jane Martin, Marilyn Murphy
Terrell, Elizabeth Thompson (research-writing); Meghan
K. Blute (research); Janet Cave (editing); Lina Baber
Burton (glossary); Barbara L. Klein (overread); Barbara
Cohen (index).

Correspondents: Maria Vincenza Aloisi (Paris), Christine
Hinze (London), Christina Lieberman (New York).
Valuable assistance was also provided by Angelika Lemmer
(Bonn).

Director of Finance: Christopher Hearing
Directors of Book Production: Marjann Caldwell,
Patricia Pascale
Director of Publishing Technology: Betsi McGrath
Director of Photography and Research: John Conrad Weiser
Director of Editorial Administration: Barbara Levitt
Manager, Technical Services: Anne Topp
Senior Production Manager: Ken Sabol
Production Manager: Virginia Reardon
Quality Assurance Manager: James King
Chief Librarian: Louise D. Forstall

Separations by the Time-Life Imaging Department.

Consultant:
Keith Michael Baker is J. E. Wallace Sterling Professor in
the Humanities and professor of history at Stanford Uni-
versity and Anthony P. Meier Family Professor and director of the Stanford Humanities Center. His research has
focused on the Enlightenment, the political culture of the
Old Regime in France, and the origins of the French
Revolution. His writings include *Condorcet: From Natural
Philosophy to Social Mathematics* and *Inventing the French
Revolution.* He also edited *The Old Regime and the French
Revolution,* a volume in the University of Chicago Read-
ings in Western Civilization, as well as *The French Revolu-
tion and the Creation of Modern Political Culture: Vol. 1, The
Political Culture of the Old Regime* and *Vol. 4, The Terror.*
Professor Baker is a member of the American Philosophi-
cal Society and the American Academy of Arts and Sci-
ences, and a Chevalier dans l'Ordre des Palmes
Académiques.

This volume is one in a series on world history that
uses contemporary art, artifacts, and personal accounts to
create an intimate portrait of daily life in the past.

Other volumes included in the *What Life Was Like* series:

On the Banks of the Nile: Egypt, 3050-30 BC
In the Age of Chivalry: Medieval Europe, AD 800-1500
When Rome Ruled the World: The Roman Empire, 100 BC-AD 200
At the Dawn of Democracy: Classical Athens, 525-322 BC
When Longships Sailed: Vikings, AD 800-1100
Among Druids and High Kings: Celtic Ireland, AD 400-1200
In the Realm of Elizabeth: England, AD 1533-1603
Amid Splendor and Intrigue: Byzantine Empire, AD 330-1453
In the Land of the Dragon: Imperial China, AD 960-1368
In the Time of War and Peace: Imperial Russia, AD 1696-1917
In the Jewel in the Crown: British India, AD 1600-1905
At the Rebirth of Genius: Renaissance Italy, AD 1400-1550
Among Samurai and Shoguns: Japan, AD 1000-1700

Other Publications:

HISTORY
Our American Century
World War II
The American Story
Voices of the Civil War
The American Indians
Lost Civilizations
Mysteries of the Unknown
Time Frame
The Civil War
Cultural Atlas

COOKING
Weight Watchers® Smart Choice Recipe Collection
Great Taste~Low Fat
Williams-Sonoma Kitchen Library

SCIENCE/NATURE
Voyage Through the Universe

DO IT YOURSELF
Total Golf
How to Fix It
The Time-Life Complete Gardener
Home Repair and Improvement
The Art of Woodworking

TIME-LIFE KIDS
Library of First Questions and Answers
A Child's First Library of Learning
I Love Math
Nature Company Discoveries
Understanding Science & Nature

For information on and a full description of any of the
Time-Life Books series listed above, please call 1-800-
621-7026 or write:

Reader Information
Time-Life Customer Service
P.O. Box C-32068
Richmond, Virginia 23261-2068

Library of Congress Cataloging-in-Publication Data
What life was like during the Age of Reason: France,
AD 1660-1800 / by the editors of Time-Life Books.
p.   cm. —
(What life was like series ; 14)
Includes bibliographical references and index.
ISBN 0-7835-5463-X
1. France—Civilization—18th century.
2. France—Social life and customs—18th century.
I. Time-Life Books.   II. Series.
DC33.4.W43 1999
944'. 034—dc21   99-28841
                                             CIP